THE
STEP-BY-STEP
BIBLE

A Panoramic Journey Through God's Word

by V. Gilbert Beers

illustrated by Dan Foote

Chariot Victor Publishing
A Division of Cook Communications

Chariot Victor Publishing
a division of Cook Communications, Colorado Springs, Colorado 80918
Cook Communications, Paris, Ontario
Kingsway Communications, Eastbourne, England

THE STEP-BY-STEP BIBLE
© 1999 by V. Gilbert Beers for text and
Cook Communications Ministries for illustrations

Cover design: Steve Diggs & Friends
Interior design: Kimberly Lovins
Creative direction: Kelly S. Robinson
Copy editor: L.B. Norton
Project editor: Kathy Davis

First printing, 1999
Printed in Singapore
03 02 01 00 99   5 4 3 2 1

Library of Congress Cataloging-in-Publication Data
Beers, V. Gilbert (Victor Gilbert), 1928-
        The step-by-step Bible : a panoramic journey through God's word /
by V. Gilbert Beers ; illustrated by Dan Foote.
    p.   cm.
        Summary: Relates the story of the Bible as one continuous narrative in chronological order, from the Creation to the early development of the Christian church.
        ISBN 0-7814-3307-X
        1. Bible stories, English. [1. Bible stories.] I. Foote, Dan, ill. II. Title.
    BS551.2.B4398   1999
    220.9'505—dc21   99-35209
                                                                      CIP

This book belongs to

_____

An Overall Look at the Bible

The Bible is the greatest story ever told. It is the story of the Greatest Person, the Lord Himself. It is also the story of God at work in the lives of His people. In the beginning, He created the world, where He has always worked in the lives of His people . . . and still does.

The story begins with the first people, Adam and Eve. They made a terrible choice in Eden and brought sin into the world. Sin grew worse until God decided to destroy all people and animals, except Noah and his family. Later, the Lord chose Abraham to be the father of the chosen people. He was one of the Patriarchs, those early people who walked with God. Abraham's grandson Jacob was the father of the twelve tribes of Israel. Jacob and his family moved to Egypt to escape famine. They lived there 400 years and became slaves.

After 400 years of slavery in Egypt, the Israelites were led to freedom by Moses. At Mount Sinai, God gave His laws to guide the nation. Later, Joshua led these people into the Promised Land and they captured much of it. For a while Israel sank into a dark period, the time of the judges, when they forgot God. Saul became their first king. When he failed, David became king, the greatest king of all.

David's son Solomon honored God at first. But he married many pagan wives who turned his heart away from the Lord. So God tore the kingdom into two parts. Ten tribes kept the name Israel; this was the Northern Kingdom. The Southern Kingdom was Judah, where Jerusalem was located. But many kings in both kingdoms were evil. They turned against the Lord. At last the Lord let the Assyrians capture Israel and take many people away. Then He let the Babylonians capture Judah and take many of their people away. Seventy years later, some came home and rebuilt Jerusalem and the Temple.

There was a period between the Old and New Testaments of about 400 years. Then Jesus was born in Bethlehem. He was the Messiah, God's Son. He worked many miracles. But most important, He died on the cross to save us from our sin. He rose from the dead, too. Some of His followers became the leaders of the new church on earth. They took the Gospel, the Good News about Jesus, all over the world.

Saul of Tarsus, later called Paul, hated Jesus at first. Then he accepted Jesus and became a great missionary. He wrote many of the books in our New Testament.

The Bible itself was completed with the writings of Paul and John. But the story of the Bible at work continues as it is preached all over the world today. You and I are part of this Bible panorama. Some day, Jesus will return to earth. He will take His followers to heaven, where we will live with Him forever. Thus, the story of the Bible is a never-ending story. When we accept Jesus as our Savior, we are part of a story that never ends. We will live forever with the Lord in His heavenly home.

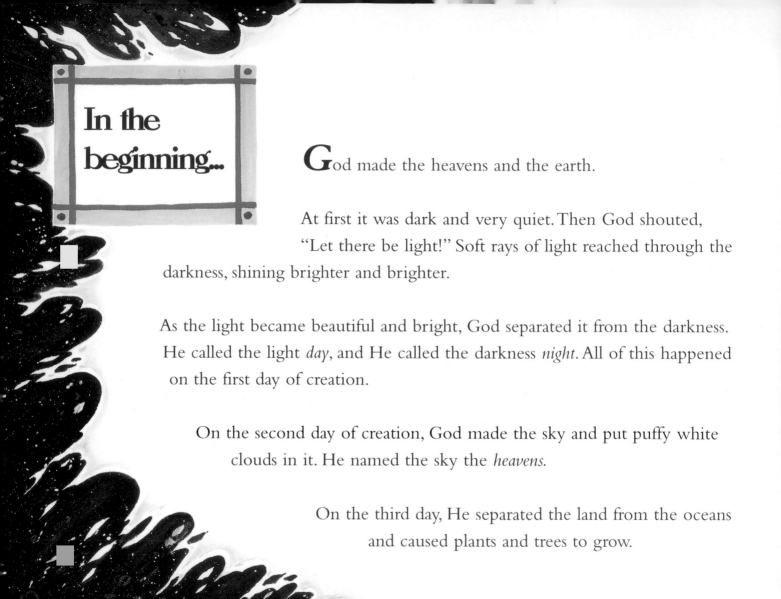

In the beginning...

God made the heavens and the earth.

At first it was dark and very quiet. Then God shouted, "Let there be light!" Soft rays of light reached through the darkness, shining brighter and brighter.

As the light became beautiful and bright, God separated it from the darkness. He called the light *day*, and He called the darkness *night*. All of this happened on the first day of creation.

On the second day of creation, God made the sky and put puffy white clouds in it. He named the sky the *heavens*.

On the third day, He separated the land from the oceans and caused plants and trees to grow.

God Creates Everything

Then God made the sun, moon, and stars. He divided the seasons into days and years. This happened on the fourth day.

Birds and fish appeared at God's command on the fifth day.

At last, on the sixth day, God made animals and filled the earth with them. Then He made a man named Adam and a woman named Eve.

On the seventh day, with His work of creation finished, God rested.

Genesis 1:1–2:3

This is the way God created Adam and Eve.

First he formed a man's body from dust, then He breathed life into it. Adam took a deep breath and became the first living person.

God gave Adam some work to do. He put him in charge of God's beautiful garden, called Eden.

"Adam needs a helper," God decided. So God made Adam go to sleep. He took one of Adam's ribs and made Eve from it.

God Makes Adam and Eve

"Eve and I are like one person," Adam said.

God planted two wonderful trees in the Garden of Eden.

One was the Tree of Life, the other was the Tree of Conscience. This second tree could help people know good and bad. But God warned Adam and Eve not to eat its fruit.

For a while, Adam and Eve lived together happily in the beautiful Garden of Eden.

Genesis 2:4-25

One day Satan came to Eve.
He wanted her to disobey God and
eat fruit from the Tree of Conscience.

"God told us not to eat that fruit," Eve said. "If
we eat it, we will die."

"That's a lie!" Satan hissed. "You won't die. You will know good and
bad, the way God does."

Eve listened to Satan and ate some of the fruit. She shared it with
Adam. Suddenly they were both ashamed. They had
disobeyed God, so they tried to hide from Him.

Adam and Eve Are Tempted

"Why are you hiding?" God asked. "Have you eaten some of that fruit?"

"Eve gave it to me," Adam quickly said.

"The snake tricked me," Eve complained.

God punished the snake, saying it must always crawl on the ground. He also punished Adam and Eve. They had to leave the Garden of Eden and never come back.

Then God sent two angels with flaming swords to guard the Tree of Life. Adam and Eve could never come near it again. If they ate fruit from that tree, they would live forever.

Now that they had sinned, it would be terrible to live forever with that sin.

Genesis 3

As time passed, Adam and Eve had two sons. Cain grew up to be a farmer and Abel a shepherd.

When it was time to give offerings to God, Cain brought some crops from his farm. Abel brought some meat from his best lambs. But something was wrong with Cain and his offering. While God was pleased with Abel's offering, He would not accept Cain's.

Cain's face became dark with anger against God.

Cain Kills Abel

"If you obey Me, your face can shine with joy," God told Cain. "But if you don't, then sin will destroy you."

Cain did not listen to God. One day he led Abel into the fields and killed him.

"Where is your brother?" God asked Cain.

"I don't keep track of my brother," Cain replied.

"But his blood is calling to Me from the ground," said God.

Then God punished Cain, saying he must wander from place to place the rest of his life. God put a mark on him so that no one would hurt him, but God would not go with him. Cain had to go through life without God.

Genesis 4:1-16

*M*any, many years went by. During this time people lived to be hundreds of years old. But as the years passed, people became so bad that God was sorry He had made them. He decided to destroy all these evil people.

There was one good man who pleased and obeyed God, and that was Noah. So God decided to keep Noah and his family safe.

"Make a boat 450 feet long, 75 feet wide, and 45 feet high," God told Noah. "Make three decks with many stalls for animals. Put a long skylight around the ship 18 inches from the top. Put a door in the side of the boat.

God also told Noah to bring animals and food on board.

Noah Builds the Ark

"I am going to cover the earth with a great flood," God said. "The flood will destroy every living thing that is not on the boat."

Noah obeyed God and did exactly what He said. It took 120 years to build this great boat, but at last it was finished.

"Go into the boat," God commanded. "Take your family and the animals with you. Take one pair of each kind of unclean animal, and seven of each kind of clean animal and bird."

Genesis 6:1–7:10

On the day the great flood began, the rain poured down in torrents. The waters under the ground gushed out. The waters went over the earth for forty days and nights, but Noah was safe on board with his wife and his three sons, Shem, Ham, and Japheth, and their wives.

Water poured over the earth, rising higher and higher until it covered the high mountains. Every person, animal, and bird outside the boat drowned.

The flood covered the earth for 150 days. Then God sent a wind, and the flood began to go away. At last the great boat came to rest on top of Mount Ararat. Three months later other mountains appeared. But it took three months more for the water to go away and the earth to dry.

At last it was time for Noah and his family to leave the boat with the animals and birds.

When he stepped outside, Noah made an altar and sacrificed some animals and birds. This was his way of saying "thank You" to God for keeping them safe.

Then God made a promise. "I will never again hurt the earth like this or destroy all living things," God promised. "As long as the earth remains, there will be springtime and harvest, cold and heat, winter and summer, day and night."

God blessed Noah and his family. He put a beautiful rainbow in the sky as a symbol of His promise. The rainbow would remind God and people that God will always keep this special promise.

Genesis 7:11–9:17

After the great flood, Noah had grandchildren and great-grandchildren. Many of them settled in the land of Babylon.

The people in this land began to plan a great city with a tall tower that would reach to the skies. They thought the tower would show how great they were.

"This will unite us and keep us together," they said. So they made bricks from clay and began to put the bricks together with tar.

But God saw what was happening. He saw how proud they were, and He was not pleased. He wanted them to think about how great He was.

The Tower of Babel

No known date

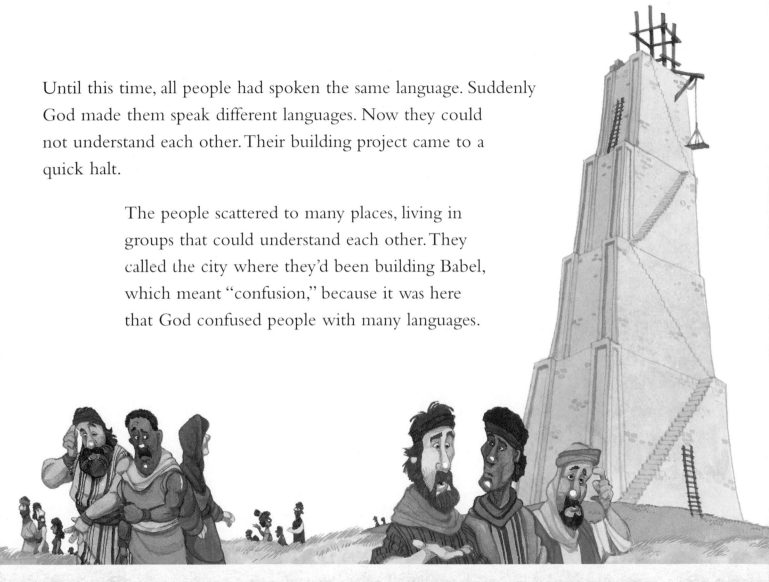

Until this time, all people had spoken the same language. Suddenly God made them speak different languages. Now they could not understand each other. Their building project came to a quick halt.

The people scattered to many places, living in groups that could understand each other. They called the city where they'd been building Babel, which meant "confusion," because it was here that God confused people with many languages.

Early civilizations include Egyptians and Sumerians

Genesis 11:1-9

Job was one of the richest men alive. He had everything: a wife, ten children, many servants, and thousands of animals. Job loved God, and God knew it. Satan knew too. One time Satan and God talked about Job. "Have you ever seen such a wonderful person?" God asked.

"Job is good because he's rich," Satan answered. "He wouldn't love You so much if You didn't give him so much. Let me take his things away, and he will curse You."

The Lord knew that Job would not do that. But He couldn't let Satan say such things. So He gave Satan permission to take Job's things away.

First outlaws attacked. They killed Job's servants and stole the animals they were guarding. Then lightning struck and killed Job's sheep and the servants guarding them. Then more outlaws came and stole more animals and killed the servants guarding them. Finally a windstorm blew down a house with all ten of Job's children in it.

"Now, watch Job curse God and die," said Satan.

The Story of Job

But he didn't. Instead Job prayed, "Lord, You have given, and You have taken away. Blessed is Your name."

"He still loves Me and honors Me," said the Lord.

"He won't if we hurt him!" said Satan. So the Lord gave Satan permission to make Job sick, with boils all over his body.

Job's wife was disgusted. "Curse God and die!" she said. Some friends came with ugly ideas. "You've sinned," they said. "That's why you have this trouble."

But Job told the Lord, "Even though You kill me, I will still trust You."

Now the Lord knew, and Satan knew, that nothing would turn Job against God. Before long Job got well. In time, he was very rich again, with twice as much as he'd had before. And more importantly, he still loved the Lord with all his heart.

*No one knows when Job lived. Many think he lived about the time of the Patriarchs, perhaps before Abraham.

The Book of Job

Noah's son Shem had many descendants. One was named Abram, who lived in the city of Ur with his wife, Sarai, and his nephew Lot.

One day God told Abram to go to the land of Canaan. "There you will become the father of a great nation," God said.

Abram obeyed God and took Sarai and Lot to Canaan. There God spoke to Abram again. "I will give this land to you and your descendants."

A great famine came to Canaan, so Abram moved with Sarai and Lot to Egypt. But he was worried. "You are very beautiful," he said to Sarai. "If the Egyptians know that you are my wife, they may kill me so they can have you.

Abram Moves to New Lands   2091 B.C.

Let's say you are my sister. Then the Egyptians will take good care of me to please you."

So that is what they did. Some of the king's helpers even told the king, called Pharaoh, about this beautiful woman. He put Sarai in his harem, where he had many other beautiful women. Pharaoh gave Abram many wonderful gifts: slaves, sheep, oxen, donkeys, and camels.

But the Lord sent a terrible disease to the people in Pharaoh's household. Somehow Pharaoh knew then that Sarai was really Abram's wife. He ordered Abram to leave Egypt with his family, but he let Abram keep all the expensive presents he had given him.

So Abram left Egypt with his family and returned to Canaan a wealthy man. Abram and Lot had so many animals that there was not enough pasture to go around. Before long Abram's herdsmen and Lot's herdsmen began to quarrel. "We're family," Abram told Lot. "We shouldn't fight among ourselves. Choose the land you want, and I'll take what's left."

When Lot was gone, the Lord gave a special promise to Abram. "You will have many, many descendants," the Lord told Abram. "I will give all this land to them."

One day four kings came down against the five kings of the land near Abram and Lot. The four defeated the five and took Lot prisoner. But one of Lot's men escaped and told

Lot Leaves Abram

the news to Abram. So Abram set out with his best fighting men and attacked the four kings at night. He defeated the four kings and captured all the loot and prisoners that they had taken, including Lot.

When Abram returned, two of the five defeated kings came out to meet him. Melchizedek, king of Salem, was like a high priest. He blessed Abram and praised God for his victory. So Abram gave Melchizedek a tenth of the loot he had captured.

The king of Sodom told Abram, "Just give me back my people. Keep all the loot from my city."

But Abram wouldn't do it. "I promised God that I would not keep one thread from your city," he said. "If I did, you would say that you had made me rich. But you may share it with those who helped me win the battle."

Genesis 13–14

One night God spoke to Abram and made a special promise to him. "Don't ever be afraid, Abram," God said. "I will protect you and take care of you."

"But what good are all the things You have given me?" Abram said. "I have no son, so someone else will inherit everything when I die. Someone else will lead my family."

"You will have a son," God promised. "Your son will get what you have."

God told Abram to look up at the star-filled sky. "Can you count the stars?" God asked. "That's how many descendants you will have. There will be too many to count."

God Makes a Promise to Abram

Abram believed God. He was a very godly man.

"I brought you away from the city of Ur," God said. "I brought you here to give you this land."

"How will I know that you will give it to me?" Abram asked.

God told Abram to prepare an offering of animals.

At sunset, God caused him to fall asleep. Abram dreamed of dark and terrible things. Then God told him of things to come. "Your descendants will be slaves for 400 years," He said. "Then they will be freed with great wealth and will come to this land to live."

Genesis 15

By this time Abram and Sarai were much too old to have children. How could God keep His promise to give them a son?

One day Sarai had an idea. She would let her servant girl Hagar and Abram have a baby. Then Sarai would take this baby as her own.

But when she knew she was going to have a baby, Hagar made fun of Sarai. This made Sarai angry and jealous.

"It's your fault," Sarai said to Abram.
"Then punish her!" said Abram.

Sarai treated Hagar so badly that Hagar ran away. But the

Sarai Is Jealous

angel of the Lord found Hagar sitting by a spring of water in the desert, weeping.

"Why are you running away?" the angel asked.

"I'm running away from Sarai," Hagar answered.

"Go home," the angel commanded. "Your baby will be a boy. You will name him Ishmael. He will be a wild one, but his descendants will become a great nation."

The angel was actually the Lord Himself. "I saw God and lived to talk about it," Hagar said.

Abram was eighty-six years old when the boy was born. As the Lord had commanded, Abram named him Ishmael.

When Abram was ninety-nine years old, God changed his name. "Your name will be Abraham, which means father of nations," God told him. God also changed Sarai's name to Sarah, which means princess.

One hot summer day Abraham was sitting by the doorway of his tent. When he saw three men coming, he ran to greet them and give them food.

"Next year I will give you and Sarah a son," one of the men said. But it wasn't a man talking. It was the Lord Himself.

Angels Visit Abraham

Sarah laughed when she heard this. She and Abraham were much too old to have a baby.

Why did Sarah laugh?" the Lord asked. "You will have a baby next year as I promised."

Sarah was afraid now. No one should doubt God, even when things seem impossible.

When the three men had rested they went on toward Sodom. Then God told Abraham that He would destroy the wicked cities of Sodom and Gomorrah. Abraham's nephew Lot lived there, so he began to plead with God. "Will you save the city for fifty good people?" Abraham asked. "What about forty, or thirty, or even ten?"

"If I find even ten good people in Sodom, I will not destroy the city," the Lord said. But Abraham wondered if God would find even ten good people in that wicked city.

Genesis 17–18

That evening, Lot was sitting by Sodom's gate. He saw two angels coming toward him, but they looked like ordinary men. So Lot stood up and welcomed them. "Stay at my house tonight," he said. "Then you can be on your way as early as you wish."

"Thanks, but we'll just sleep here on the street," the angels answered. Lot knew that was not safe, so he kept urging them to come home with him. When they did, he gave them a wonderful dinner. But about bedtime, the men of Sodom surrounded Lot's house. "Bring those men out here," they demanded. "We want to abuse them."

"These men are my guests. Don't hurt them!" Lot protested. But the men of Sodom became violent and began to break the door down.

God Destroys Sodom and Gomorrah with Fire

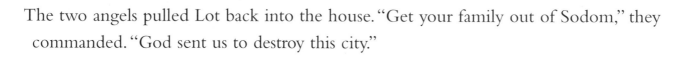

The two angels pulled Lot back into the house. "Get your family out of Sodom," they commanded. "God sent us to destroy this city."

When Lot tried to stay, the angels grabbed him and his family by their hands and rushed them out of the city. "Run! Don't look back!" the angels shouted. "Run to the mountains." But as they ran, Lot's wife looked back. Because she disobeyed, she became a pillar of salt.

As the sun was rising, God sent fire like rain on Sodom and Gomorrah. Everything in and around these cities was destroyed. As Abraham looked toward the two cities the next morning, he saw smoke rising up into the sky. But Lot and his daughters were safe. Abraham's prayers had saved them.

Genesis 19:1-29

*M*ost people don't have new babies when they are 100, but Abraham did. He and Sarah had dreamed of having a son. Now when they were old, Isaac was born.

But Sarah was jealous of Abraham's other son, Ishmael. She demanded that Abraham send Hagar and Ishmael away. Of course this made Abraham very sad, but God told him to do it. He would take care of Hagar and Ishmael.

Isaac grew to be a handsome, strong young man. Then one day God tested Abraham's faith and obedience to Him. "Go to the land of Moriah," God said. "Sacrifice Isaac as a burnt offering on an altar."

Abraham was confused and sad. How could Isaac become the father of a great nation if he was sacrificed? But Abraham trusted God completely. He made the altar and put

Abraham Offers Isaac

2066 B.C. Isaac is born

|

wood on it. Then he tied Isaac and laid him on the altar. He even raised the knife in his hand.

"Abraham!" God shouted. "Don't hurt Isaac. I know now that you will obey Me completely." God showed Abraham a ram caught in some bushes, and Abraham sacrificed the ram instead.

"Because you have obeyed Me completely, I will bless you," God said. "Your descendants will be many, like the stars in the sky and the sand on the seashore. They will be a blessing to all nations."

Genesis 22:1-19

During the time of Abraham, young people didn't have dates, fall in love, and get married as people do now. Most parents decided whom their children would marry.

Abraham didn't want his son to marry a local girl from an ungodly tribe. But where would he find a bride for Isaac? He couldn't leave his tribe to look for one. So Abraham called for his oldest and most trusted servant.

"Go to my relatives back in Haran," Abraham told him. "Find a wife for Isaac there."

The servant loaded ten camels with presents and set off. After many days he stopped at a spring of water. "Lord, show me who should

Isaac Finds His Bride

become Isaac's wife," the servant begged. "When I ask for a drink of water, let her say that she will also water my camels."

He was still praying when a young woman came to the spring. When the servant asked for a drink, she said, "Let me also water your camels." Then the servant knew he had found Isaac's bride.

The servant was so happy to learn that Rebekah was one of Abraham's close relatives. She took him to see her father, Bethuel.

When Abraham's servant told how God had guided him to Rebekah, the whole family knew that Rebekah should go back to marry Isaac. And even though Isaac had never had one date with Rebekah, he loved her very, very much.

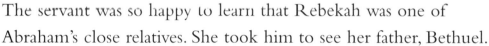

Genesis 24

Isaac was forty when he married Rebekah. But after many years, they still had no children. They begged God for a child. At last, when Isaac was sixty, he and Rebekah had twin boys. Esau had red hair, almost like fur. He became a great hunter and was Isaac's favorite son. Jacob was quiet and worked around home. He was Rebekah's favorite.

Since Esau was older, he had the birthright, which meant he would be the head of the family when Isaac died.

One day Jacob was cooking some stew when Esau came home from hunting. Esau had found nothing and was very hungry.

Esau Sells His Birthright to Jacob
2006 B.C. Jacob and Esau are born

1

"Give me some of that stew," said Esau.

"Give me your birthright," said Jacob.

At that moment Esau didn't care about such things. He just wanted something to eat. So he vowed before God that he would trade his birthright for a bowl of stew.

Esau ate his stew and walked away, not even thinking about what he had given up.

2000 B.C. King Minos of Crete makes first interior bathroom

Genesis 25:19-34

Isaac was a peace-loving man, as you will see from this story.

It all began with a wonderful year. Isaac's crops were great. God was blessing him, so he became rich. But his Philistine neighbors were jealous. They filled Isaac's wells with dirt.

"Go away!" Abimelech, king of the Philistines, said to Isaac. "You're too rich and powerful for us."

So Isaac moved to another place and dug out the wells that Abraham had once used.

Isaac Gives Up His Wells

"This is our land," some Philistine neighbors said. "This is our well."

Rather than fight, Isaac dug a new well. But the Philistines fought and argued about that one too. So Isaac and his men dug yet another new well. This time the Philistines left him alone.

"At last we can live here in peace," said Isaac.

So you can see that Isaac was a very peaceful man.
He would rather move and dig new wells
than fight.

Genesis 26:12-33

*I*saac grew old and was nearly blind. One day he asked Esau to come to him. "Hunt for some venison and prepare it the way I like it. After I eat, I will give you my blessing. Then you will lead this family when I die."

Isaac did not know that years before Esau had sold his birthright to Jacob for a bowl of stew. Isaac also did not know that Rebekah had overheard his instructions to Esau. She quickly ran to tell Jacob.

"Hurry! Get some young goats, and I will cook them the way your father likes. When you take the meat to him, he will give you the blessing."

Jacob Tricks Isaac

Rebekah put Esau's clothes on Jacob so he would smell like Esau. She put hairy skin from the young goats on his arms and neck so he would feel hairy like Esau.

Jacob took the meat to Isaac. At first Isaac was suspicious, but when he smelled the clothes and felt the hairy skin, he ate the food and gave Jacob his blessing.

Then Esau arrived and asked for Isaac's blessing. Now Isaac knew he had been tricked. Esau knew too and he was angry with Jacob, but it was too late. Isaac could not take the blessing back. Jacob would lead the family when Isaac died.

Genesis 27:1-40

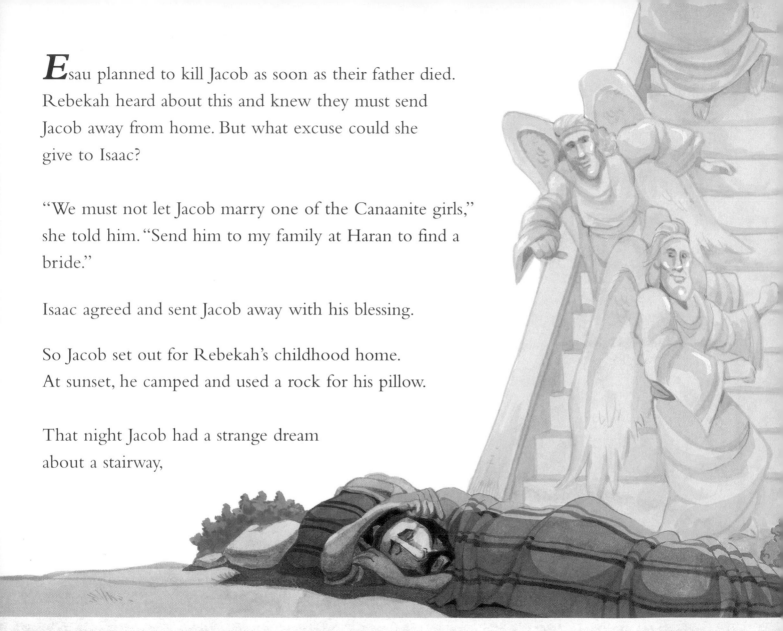

*E*sau planned to kill Jacob as soon as their father died. Rebekah heard about this and knew they must send Jacob away from home. But what excuse could she give to Isaac?

"We must not let Jacob marry one of the Canaanite girls," she told him. "Send him to my family at Haran to find a bride."

Isaac agreed and sent Jacob away with his blessing.

So Jacob set out for Rebekah's childhood home. At sunset, he camped and used a rock for his pillow.

That night Jacob had a strange dream about a stairway,

Jacob's Ladder

1929 B.C. Jacob runs away to Haran

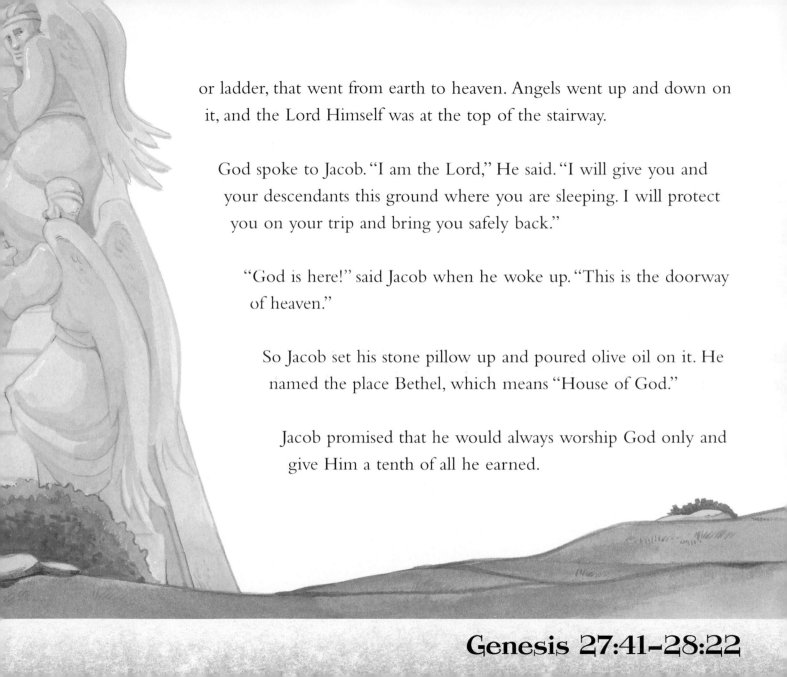

or ladder, that went from earth to heaven. Angels went up and down on it, and the Lord Himself was at the top of the stairway.

God spoke to Jacob. "I am the Lord," He said. "I will give you and your descendants this ground where you are sleeping. I will protect you on your trip and bring you safely back."

"God is here!" said Jacob when he woke up. "This is the doorway of heaven."

So Jacob set his stone pillow up and poured olive oil on it. He named the place Bethel, which means "House of God."

Jacob promised that he would always worship God only and give Him a tenth of all he earned.

Genesis 27:41–28:22

At last Jacob came to Haran, where his mother had grown up. He found some shepherds lying near a well covered by a big stone. "Do you know my uncle Laban?" he asked. Laban was the brother of Jacob's mother, Rebekah.

"Of course," the shepherds said. "Here comes his daughter Rachel with some sheep."

Jacob rolled away the stone covering the well and helped Rachel water her sheep. When he told her who he was, she took Jacob home to meet her family.

"I'll work for you seven years if I can marry Rachel," Jacob told his uncle.

Jacob Marries Rachel

Jacob and Laban made a deal, but Laban tricked Jacob. On the wedding night Laban brought Leah, Rachel's older sister, for Jacob to marry. In those days brides wore veils over their faces, so Jacob married Leah without knowing it. When he realized the truth the next morning, Jacob was very angry.

"In our country, you must marry the older sister first," Laban said. "You can now marry Rachel, but you must work for me another seven years."

That's the way it was with Jacob and his uncle. Laban was always finding a way to cheat Jacob.

As the years passed, Jacob had eleven sons and one daughter. But Jacob was not happy there with Laban. He wanted to go home.

Genesis 29:1-28

I want to take my family and go home," Jacob told Laban.

But Laban did not want Jacob to leave. Since Jacob had come, Laban had become a rich man with many animals. He knew God had blessed him because of Jacob.

"How can I keep you here?" he asked. "Give me all the sheep and goats that are not pure white," Jacob answered. So that's what Laban did. Now Jacob had a flock with black and spotted animals, while Laban's flocks were pure white.

Now it was Jacob who tricked Laban. He caused Laban's white animals to have little ones with his black and spotted animals. Of course the babies were mostly black or spotted, so Jacob's flocks grew and Laban's did not. Laban and his sons were very angry.

Jacob Runs Away

One day God spoke to Jacob. "Go home!" He said. So Jacob ran away, secretly taking his wives and his twelve children and servants and animals. When Laban found out that Jacob and his family had left, he chased them. But God warned Laban in a dream not to hurt them.

When Laban caught up with Jacob, the two of them laid up a pile of stones. "We will not pass by this pile of stones to hurt each other," they said. Laban kissed his daughters and grandchildren and went home. Then Jacob and his family went on toward Jacob's childhood home.

Genesis 30:25–31:55

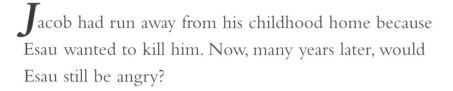

Jacob had run away from his childhood home because Esau wanted to kill him. Now, many years later, would Esau still be angry?

Jacob sent some messengers ahead to find out. "Please, let's be friends," was Jacob's plea. But the messengers came back with bad news: Esau was coming with an army of 400 men.

Jacob prayed for God to protect him. Then he sent hundreds of animals to Esau as a gift.

That night, Jacob sent his family and belongings across the river. All through the night Jacob wrestled with an angel, who was actually God.

Jacob Meets Esau

Toward morning, God gave Jacob a new name. From now on, he would be called Israel.

Esau came the next day. But instead of killing Jacob, he hugged him and kissed him.

Esau went back home with his army, and Jacob and his family followed behind. Jacob knew that God had protected him and brought him back safely as He had promised.

As Jacob moved slowly toward his childhood home, he stopped at Bethel, the place where he had dreamed about a stairway to heaven. There God reminded Jacob of his new name. God said He would give Jacob the land where he was staying and promised that he would have many descendants.

The next stop on the trip south was Bethlehem. There Rachel had a baby boy—Benjamin, Jacob's twelfth son. But Rachel died and was buried there.

Genesis 32–33; 35:1-20

*A*t last Jacob and his family arrived at his father Isaac's home.

They had not been there long before Isaac died.

Soon after that Esau and his family moved away, because there was not enough pastureland for himself and Jacob.

There Jacob's twelve sons grew to be young men.

But Joseph became Jacob's favorite son, which made the other brothers jealous. Jacob even made a special brightly colored cloak for Joseph to wear.

Joseph's Brothers Sell Him

Joseph dreamed some strange dreams and told his family about them.

The dreams seemed to say that Joseph's family would bow down before him someday; naturally this idea made Joseph's brothers angry.

One day Jacob sent Joseph out to the far pastures to see how his brothers were doing.

But the jealous brothers grabbed Joseph and sold him as a slave to some traders headed for Egypt.

Then they tore Joseph's cloak and put the blood of a goat on it. When Jacob saw the stained, torn cloak, he was sure that a wild animal had killed his favorite son.

1900 B.C. Wheel with spokes invented in the Near East

Genesis 37:1-33

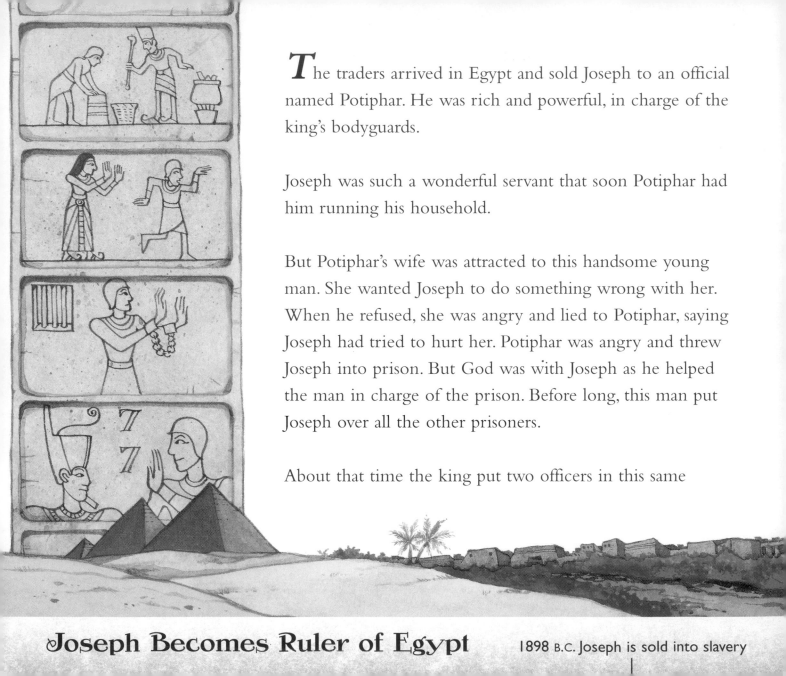

The traders arrived in Egypt and sold Joseph to an official named Potiphar. He was rich and powerful, in charge of the king's bodyguards.

Joseph was such a wonderful servant that soon Potiphar had him running his household.

But Potiphar's wife was attracted to this handsome young man. She wanted Joseph to do something wrong with her. When he refused, she was angry and lied to Potiphar, saying Joseph had tried to hurt her. Potiphar was angry and threw Joseph into prison. But God was with Joseph as he helped the man in charge of the prison. Before long, this man put Joseph over all the other prisoners.

About that time the king put two officers in this same

Joseph Becomes Ruler of Egypt

1898 B.C. Joseph is sold into slavery

prison. One night they both had strange dreams. They were surprised that Joseph could tell them what their dreams meant. Joseph predicted that one servant would be executed and the other returned to his job, and that's just what happened.

Years went by, and one night the king had strange dreams. No one knew what they meant.

Then the servant who had gone back to his job remembered Joseph and told the king about him.

The king called for Joseph, who told him exactly what his dreams meant: Egypt would have seven wonderful years, followed by seven years of famine.

The king knew that God was helping Joseph. So he made Joseph ruler of all Egypt, to prepare for the coming famine.

1885 B.C. Joseph becomes ruler of Egypt

Genesis 37:36; 39:1–41:57

*T*here were seven years of good crops, just as God had said.

Each year Joseph stored part of Egypt's grain in cities throughout the land. At last all the grain barns were full.

Then the famine came. Crops did not grow. No one had food to eat, just as God had said. But Joseph had stored enough grain for everyone.

When people begged the king to help them, he sent them to Joseph. Joseph sold grain to the Egyptians and to people from nearby countries.

As time passed, Jacob sent Joseph's ten older brothers to Egypt to buy grain.

Joseph's Brothers Buy Grain from Him

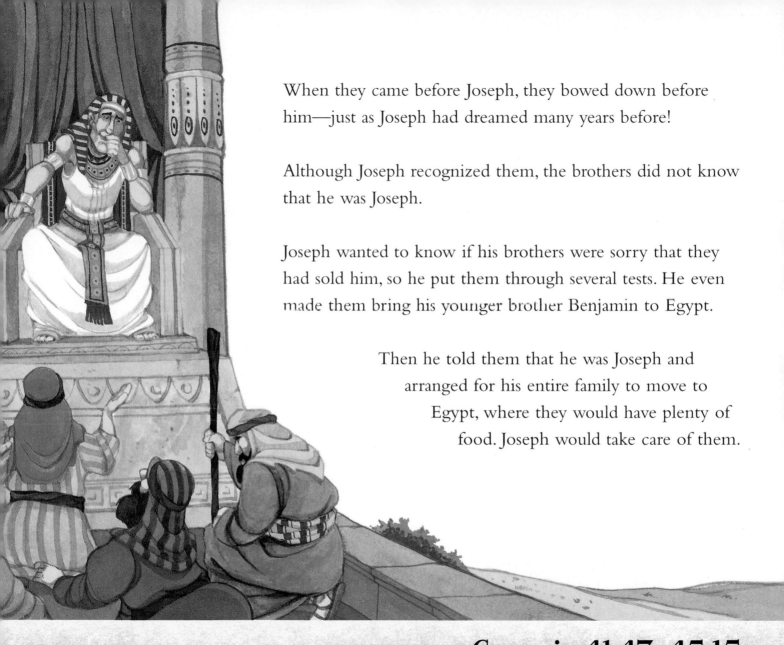

When they came before Joseph, they bowed down before him—just as Joseph had dreamed many years before!

Although Joseph recognized them, the brothers did not know that he was Joseph.

Joseph wanted to know if his brothers were sorry that they had sold him, so he put them through several tests. He even made them bring his younger brother Benjamin to Egypt.

Then he told them that he was Joseph and arranged for his entire family to move to Egypt, where they would have plenty of food. Joseph would take care of them.

Genesis 41:47–45:15

*J*acob was certainly surprised to hear that Joseph was alive and ruler over Egypt.

One night God spoke to Jacob. "Don't be afraid to go to Egypt to live," God said. "Someday all your descendants will come back home."

Soon Jacob and all his family were on their way to Egypt with everything they owned.

When Jacob saw Joseph, they hugged each other and cried. Pharaoh gave Joseph's family the best land in the region, called Goshen. Through all the years of famine, they had plenty of food. The people of Egypt had plenty of food too. But they had to buy it.

Before long, the king owned everything in the land. But the people did not complain. They were happy to have food to eat.

Joseph's Family Lives in Egypt

1805 B.C. Joseph dies

Just before Jacob died, he blessed all his sons. He gave a special blessing to Joseph and his two sons.

After Jacob died, Joseph's brothers were afraid. They thought that now Joseph would get even with them for selling him.

"Don't be afraid," Joseph told them. "God brought me to Egypt to save our family from famine. I will take care of you."

So Joseph's family lived in Egypt for many years. They had plenty of food and everything else they needed. Joseph was 110 when he died. But his family continued to live in Egypt for many more years.

*J*acob's descendants lived in Egypt for 400 years. The king who knew and loved Joseph grew old and died. So did the kings who took his place. At last there was a king who didn't know or care about a man named Joseph who had long ago saved Egypt from starving.

This king, called Pharaoh, was afraid of the Israelites, Jacob's descendants. "There are too many of them," he complained. "If we have war, they might help the enemy." So he made the Israelites his slaves. They worked hard for Pharaoh.

The Israelites had many children. Pharaoh did not like this. He tried to kill their babies when they were born, but God protected them.

One of these babies was Moses. His mother was afraid he would be killed, so she hid

The Hebrews Become Slaves

1700 B.C. Stonehenge, England

him at home for three months. Then she made a little basket and put Moses in it. She hid the basket by the river.

One of Pharaoh's daughters came to the river to bathe. She found baby Moses and decided to keep him. Miriam, Moses' big sister, saw this. She ran to the princess and asked, "Shall I find someone to take care of him for you?"

"Yes," said the princess. "I will pay her well."

So Moses' own mother took care of baby Moses until he was older. Then she brought him to the princess.

1526 B.C. Moses is born

Exodus 1:1–2:10

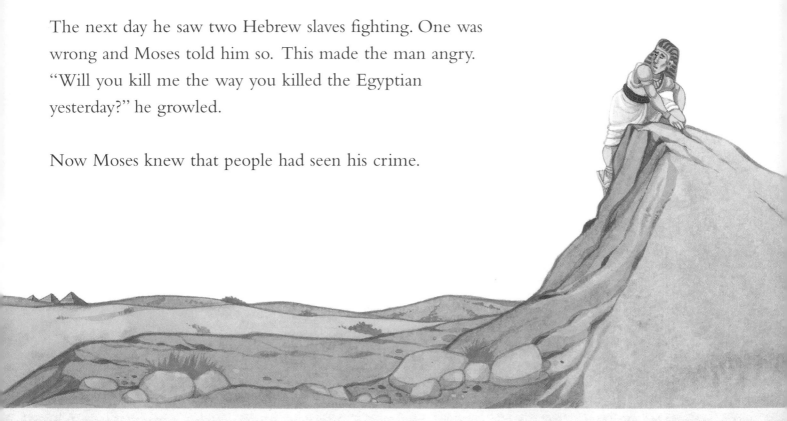

Baby Moses grew up to be a strong prince of Egypt. Somehow he knew that he was really a Hebrew, one of the Israelites.

One day Moses was watching Hebrew slaves at work. He saw an Egyptian knock a slave down. Moses killed the Egyptian and buried him in the sand.

The next day he saw two Hebrew slaves fighting. One was wrong and Moses told him so. This made the man angry. "Will you kill me the way you killed the Egyptian yesterday?" he growled.

Now Moses knew that people had seen his crime.

Moses Runs Away

1550–1200 B.C. Late Bronze Age

Even the king knew and gave orders for Moses to be arrested and killed. So Moses ran far away to the land of Midian.

One day in Midian Moses sat by a well. Some shepherd girls brought their sheep for water, but other shepherds chased the girls away. When Moses saw that, he was angry. He chased those selfish shepherds away and helped the girls water their sheep.

The girls told their father, Jethro, what had happened, and Jethro invited Moses to live with them. Eventually Moses married Zipporah, one of Jethro's daughters. They had a son named Gershom.

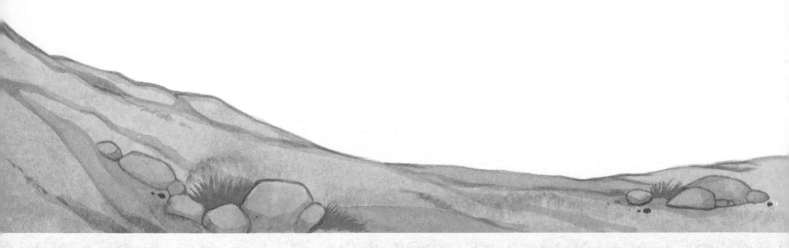

Exodus 2:11-22

One day Moses was near Mount Horeb, the mountain of God, taking care of Jethro's sheep. Suddenly he saw a bush that was on fire but never burned up.

God spoke to Moses from this bush. "Don't come any closer," He warned. "Take off your shoes. You are on holy ground. I am the God of your ancestors Abraham, Isaac, and Jacob."

Moses was afraid to look, so he covered his face with his hands.

"I will take My people from their slavery in Egypt," God said, "and bring them to a good land with plenty of food. I am

The Burning Bush

sending you to demand that Pharaoh let My people go."

Moses didn't want this job, and he argued with God.
"I'm not the right person," he said.

But God answered, "I will be with you. You will lead the people back here to worship Me."

Moses kept making excuses. "The people will ask which God has sent me." "They won't believe me." "I can't speak well."

At last God said to Moses, "Your brother Aaron is coming to see you. He will help."

So Moses took his wife and sons and headed for Egypt with Aaron. When they arrived, Moses and Aaron called the Israelite leaders together and told them God would set them free.

Exodus 3:1–4:31

Moses and Aaron went to Pharaoh and demanded, "Let our people go. God says you must."

Pharaoh was not impressed. "Who is this God?" he asked. "I don't know Him. No, I will not let your people go."

Then Pharaoh made the slaves work even harder. They had to make bricks without straw.

Moses complained to God, but God sent him back to Pharaoh. This time Moses and Aaron performed a miracle.

When Aaron threw his rod to the ground it became a snake. Pharaoh's magicians did the same thing. Then Aaron's snake swallowed the magicians' snakes. But Pharaoh still said no.

Moses Shows Pharaoh Many Miracles

The next day Moses and Aaron came back, and when Aaron pointed his rod toward the Nile River, it became blood. And Pharaoh still said no.

The Lord continued to do new miracles through Moses and Aaron. One day frogs came over all the land. Another time lice covered the Egyptians and their animals. Then a terrible disease killed many Egyptian cattle. But each time, Pharaoh said no. He would not let the people go.

Boils came over the people and animals. A terrible hailstorm killed many people and animals. Locusts swarmed over the land, destroying everything that was left. At last Pharaoh shouted at Moses, "Go away! I don't ever want to see you again."

"All right," Moses said. "You will never see me again."

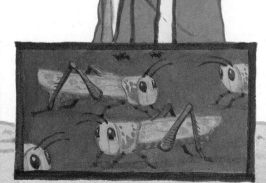

Exodus 5:1–10:29

*E*ach time the Lord did a great miracle, Moses became more famous throughout Egypt. By this time the Egyptians were sure that God was on the side of the Israelites.

"Tell the Israelites to ask their Egyptian neighbors for gold and other precious things," God told Moses. "I will do one more miracle. After that, Pharaoh will really want the Israelites to leave."

Moses sent word to Pharaoh. "About midnight the Lord will go through Egypt.
Every oldest son will die, even yours. But not one Israelite son will die."
Still Pharaoh did not back down.

The Passover

Then the Lord gave special instructions to the Israelites. "Put the blood of a lamb on the sides of your door frames," He ordered. "Also put the blood on the panel above the door. Eat roast lamb with your traveling clothes on. This will be called Passover, because the Lord will pass over the homes with blood by the door."

The Israelites obeyed the Lord. That night, at midnight, all firstborn Egyptian sons died, but not one Israelite son died. The Egyptians were terrified.

Now the Israelites asked their Egyptian neighbors for gold and other valuable things. The Egyptians gave them everything they wanted, and Pharaoh at last ordered the Israelites to leave.

Exodus 11:1–12:36

It was the middle of the night when Pharaoh ordered the Israelites out of Egypt.

The Israelites took what they owned and left their homes. There were about a million people, as well as their animals. What a sight that was!

That night the Lord led His people from slavery in Egypt. This all happened exactly 430 years after Jacob's family had come to Egypt to be with Joseph and escape the famine.

The Exodus from Egypt   1446 B.C.

This special night was called the Passover, for the Lord had passed over the homes with blood around the door. From now on, the Israelite people would celebrate Passover each year. They would follow the rules the Lord gave them.

"Remember this special day forever," the Lord commanded. "Remember it every year at this time. Tell your children why you are celebrating this Passover. Remember also that I will bring you now to a new land." Because it was the land the Lord promised to His people, it has often been called the Promised Land.

Exodus 12:37–13:16

The Israelites were free at last. They would never be Pharaoh's slaves again.

They set out for their new home, taking the bones of Joseph with them as their ancestors had promised to do.

The shortest way to the Promised Land was through the land of the Philistines. But going that way would certainly start a war with the people who lived there, so the Lord led them around the Philistine lands toward Mount Sinai instead.

Pillars of Cloud and Fire

God knew that the Israelites were not yet prepared to fight a war. They could get discouraged and want to go back to Egypt.

During the day, God led the Israelites with a pillar of cloud. At night, He led them with a pillar of fire.

The pillar of cloud or pillar of fire was always there. It never left them. So the Israelites knew that God Himself was always with them and would lead them every step of the way.

Exodus 13:17-22

After Pharaoh let the Israelites go, he changed his mind. He didn't want to lose all those slaves. So he came after the Israelites with 600 of his best chariots and drivers. The Israelites were headed right toward the Red Sea.

"Tell the people to camp along the shore of the sea," God said to Moses. "Pharaoh will think you are trapped and will chase you. Then I will show him that I am the Lord."

So the Israelites camped where God said. When they saw Pharaoh's army coming, they were terrified. They turned against Moses. "It would be better to be slaves in Egypt than die here!"

"Don't be afraid," Moses said. "The Lord will fight for you."

Crossing the Red Sea

"Hold your rod toward the sea," the Lord said.

When Moses did that, the waters moved apart, making a path through the sea. The Israelites walked across on dry land, a wall of water on each side.

When the Israelites were safe on the other side, and the Egyptians were coming after them on the path through the sea, Moses held his rod out again. The walls of water came crashing down on the Egyptians and their chariots.

The Israelites realized that God had done this great miracle for them. They worshiped the Lord and sang praises to Him. And they trusted His servant Moses.

Exodus 14:1–15:21

From the Red Sea, Moses led the people into the Wilderness of Shur. But for the next three days they had no water. At last they found water at Marah, but it was so bitter they could not drink it.

The people were angry with Moses. "Must we die of thirst?" they grumbled.

Moses begged the Lord for help. The Lord showed him a special tree. When Moses threw a branch from it into the water, the water became sweet.

"Listen to Me," the Lord commanded. "Obey Me!"

But awhile later the Israelites were grumbling again. "We have no food here! We wish we were back in Egypt."

Food and Water Problems in the Desert

That evening hundreds of quail came down. Now the Israelites had meat to eat. The next morning white flakes called manna appeared on the ground. They didn't know it then, but God would provide this special food for them for the next forty years.

Later the people had another water shortage. Once more they complained and Moses prayed.

The Lord sent Moses out to a rock at Mount Horeb. "Strike the rock with your rod," He commanded.

When Moses did that, water gushed out. Now the people had more than enough food and water.

Exodus 15:22–17:7

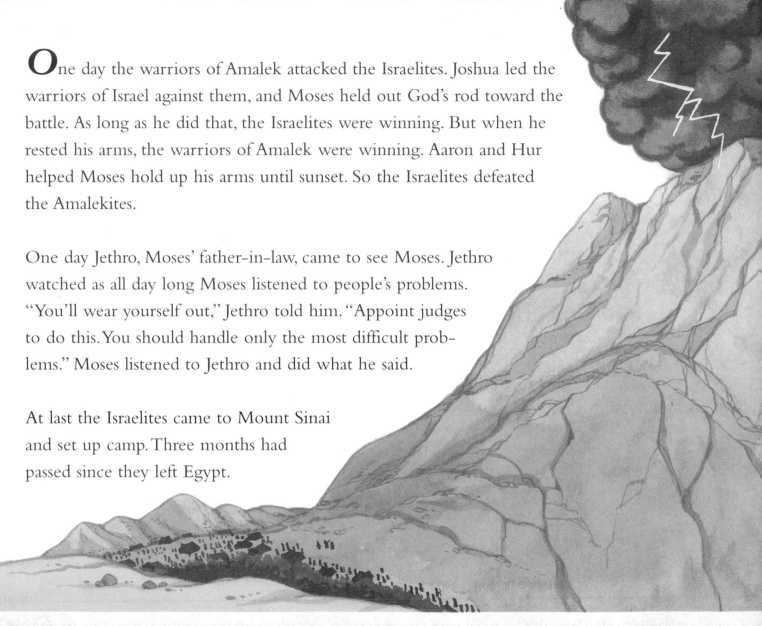

One day the warriors of Amalek attacked the Israelites. Joshua led the warriors of Israel against them, and Moses held out God's rod toward the battle. As long as he did that, the Israelites were winning. But when he rested his arms, the warriors of Amalek were winning. Aaron and Hur helped Moses hold up his arms until sunset. So the Israelites defeated the Amalekites.

One day Jethro, Moses' father-in-law, came to see Moses. Jethro watched as all day long Moses listened to people's problems. "You'll wear yourself out," Jethro told him. "Appoint judges to do this. You should handle only the most difficult problems." Moses listened to Jethro and did what he said.

At last the Israelites came to Mount Sinai and set up camp. Three months had passed since they left Egypt.

The Ten Commandments and Other Rules

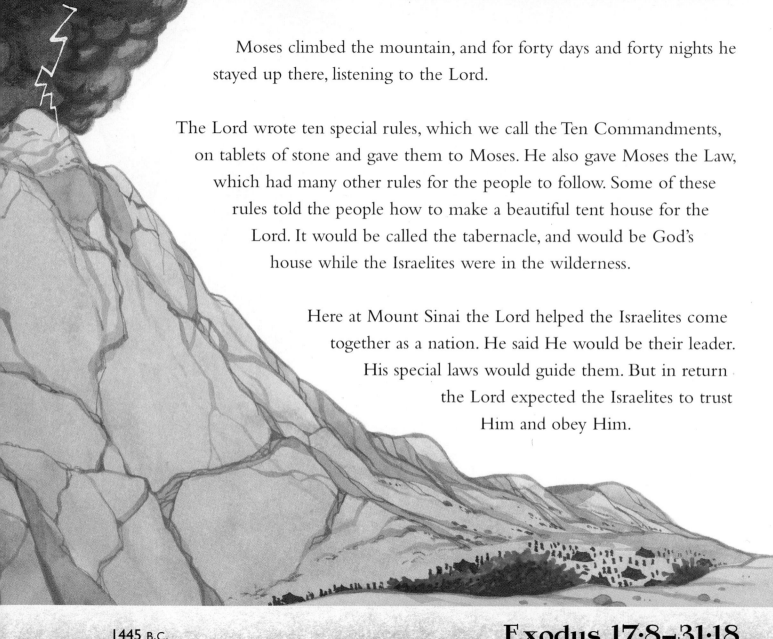

Moses climbed the mountain, and for forty days and forty nights he stayed up there, listening to the Lord.

The Lord wrote ten special rules, which we call the Ten Commandments, on tablets of stone and gave them to Moses. He also gave Moses the Law, which had many other rules for the people to follow. Some of these rules told the people how to make a beautiful tent house for the Lord. It would be called the tabernacle, and would be God's house while the Israelites were in the wilderness.

Here at Mount Sinai the Lord helped the Israelites come together as a nation. He said He would be their leader. His special laws would guide them. But in return the Lord expected the Israelites to trust Him and obey Him.

1445 B.C.

Exodus 17:8–31:18

The Israelites became restless waiting for Moses to come down from Mount Sinai. At last they could wait no longer.

"Something has happened to Moses," they complained to Moses' brother, Aaron. "Make a god to lead us through the wilderness."

"Give me your golden earrings," said Aaron. He melted their gold jewelry and formed a golden calf.

Then the people cried out, "This is the god that led us out of Egypt."

The Golden Calf

The next day Aaron prepared a big feast that turned into a wild party with people doing many evil things. The Lord was very angry. "I will destroy them!" He said.

"Please don't do that," Moses begged. "The Egyptians will say you brought the Israelites here to kill them." So the Lord listened to Moses.

When Moses got back to camp he was furious. He threw down the stone tablets God had given him, breaking them into pieces. Then he ground up the golden calf, spread the golden powder on the water, and made the people drink it.

Moses ordered some of the people put to death. Then the Lord sent a great plague to punish more of them. Now the people were sorry they had sinned by making the golden calf.

Exodus 32

Moses went back onto Mount Sinai to talk with the Lord for another forty days. The Lord gave Moses two more tablets like the ones he had broken, and more rules for the people.

When Moses came back to camp, he asked the people for gifts to be used in making the tabernacle, God's tent house in the wilderness. The people were very generous and gave wonderful gifts—gold, silver, bronze, animal skins, and wood. They gave so much that Moses had to tell them to stop giving.

Then people with special abilities were appointed to do the work. Weavers put animal skins and blue, purple, and red linens together. Frames were made of acacia wood. Poles were covered with gold and set into silver bases. Craftsmen made a golden box called the ark to hold the stone tablets. They also made a special golden table, a golden lampstand, and two altars. They made a beautiful large bowl called the laver where the priests washed. They made

The Tabernacle

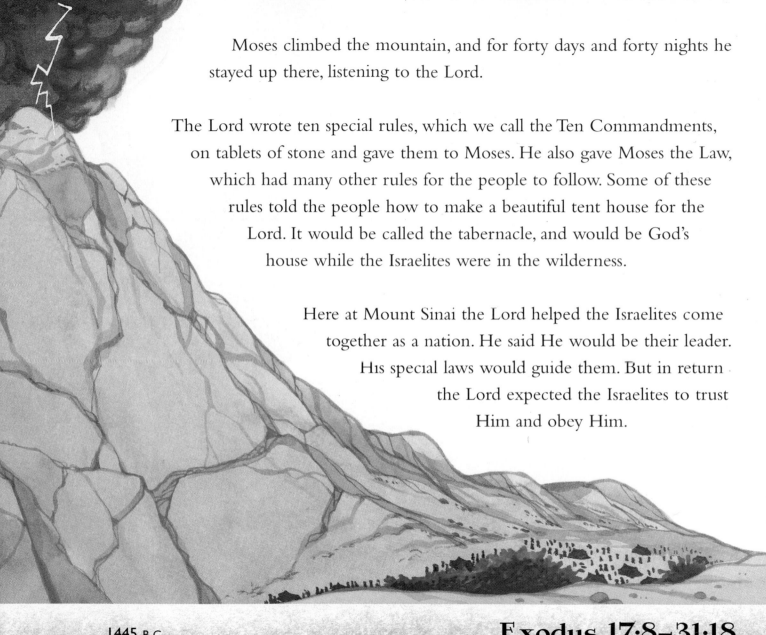

Moses climbed the mountain, and for forty days and forty nights he stayed up there, listening to the Lord.

The Lord wrote ten special rules, which we call the Ten Commandments, on tablets of stone and gave them to Moses. He also gave Moses the Law, which had many other rules for the people to follow. Some of these rules told the people how to make a beautiful tent house for the Lord. It would be called the tabernacle, and would be God's house while the Israelites were in the wilderness.

Here at Mount Sinai the Lord helped the Israelites come together as a nation. He said He would be their leader. His special laws would guide them. But in return the Lord expected the Israelites to trust Him and obey Him.

1445 B.C.

Exodus 17:8–31:18

The Israelites became restless waiting for Moses to come down from Mount Sinai. At last they could wait no longer.

"Something has happened to Moses," they complained to Moses' brother, Aaron. "Make a god to lead us through the wilderness."

"Give me your golden earrings," said Aaron. He melted their gold jewelry and formed a golden calf.

Then the people cried out, "This is the god that led us out of Egypt."

The Golden Calf

special clothing which the Lord
designed for the priests to wear.
The people made the tabernacle
exactly as the Lord had said.

The cloud with the Lord's presence
covered the tabernacle, and the glory
of the Lord filled the tent.

When the cloud stayed in one place,
the people stayed. When the
cloud moved, the people
moved too.

Exodus 34:1–40:38

The Lord led His people out of slavery in Egypt. He led them through the wilderness to Mount Sinai. He gave them Ten Commandments and the rest of the Law to guide them. He gave them plans for His tent house, the tabernacle. He chose the Levites, descendants of Levi, to be His priests.

The Book of Leviticus gives the Lord's laws about the work of the priests, the offerings they made, the great feasts, and many other things. The Book of Numbers tells about the long trip from Mount Sinai to the Promised Land.

God Prepares His People to Become a Great Nation

The twelve tribes camped and moved the way the Lord told them to until at last they came to the wilderness at Paran. There Moses sent twelve spies into the Promised Land.

The spies went throughout the land. At the Valley of Eschol they cut a large bunch of grapes—so large that two men had to carry it back on a pole.

After forty days the spies returned to camp. They told Moses and the other Israelites about the wonderful, rich land. But they also reported that they had seen walled cities and powerful people. Most of the spies were afraid, because they thought the people in this new land were too powerful to fight.

Then the rest of the Israelites were afraid too. They forgot that the Lord would help them.

Leviticus 1:1–Numbers 13:33

When the Israelites heard the spies' report, they started whining and complaining once again. "It would be better to die in Egypt. We'll all be killed here. Our wives and children will be slaves. Let's choose a new leader to take us back."

Then two of the spies, Joshua and Caleb, spoke up. "The land God promised is a wonderful land," they said. "Don't be afraid. The Lord loves us and will take us safely into the land. Don't rebel against Him."

But the Israelites wouldn't listen.

The Lord was angry with His people, but once again Moses begged the Lord to forgive them.

The People Rebel Again

Then the Lord answered, "These people have seen all My great miracles, but still they rebel against Me. This generation will stay in the wilderness until they die over the next forty years. Only Joshua and Caleb will go into the Promised Land."

When the Lord finished talking, the ten spies who had frightened the people suddenly died. Joshua and Caleb remained alive.

Some of the people realized now that they had made the Lord angry, so they became determined to go fight for the Promised Land.

"Don't do it!" Moses warned. "The Lord is not with you." But they went anyway. Of course the enemies chased them far away. It was too late. They could not win, because the Lord was not helping them now.

Numbers 14

The Israelites kept on rebelling. One day three men named Korah, Dathan, and Abiram turned against Moses. The Lord opened a large crack in the ground, which swallowed them. Then the people grumbled about that, so the Lord sent a great plague to punish them. Thousands of people died.

One time Moses himself disobeyed the Lord. The Israelites were camped at Kadesh, but there was not enough water. Once more the people complained and turned against their leaders. So Moses and Aaron went to the doorway of the tabernacle and prayed.

Moses Disobeys God

"Speak to that rock over there," the Lord commanded. "Tell it to pour out water for the people."

Moses called the people together. "Must we bring water from this rock for you?" he asked. Moses lifted Aaron's rod. But he did not do what the Lord had said. Instead of speaking to the rock, he hit it twice. Water poured out of it.

God said to Moses and Aaron, "You did not honor Me before the people. Therefore you will not lead them into the Promised Land. You will die before they go in."

Moses and Aaron knew they had made a terrible mistake, but it was too late. Moses had disobeyed the Lord. They accepted their punishment without complaining.

Numbers 16:1–20:13

oses sent messengers to the King of Edom to ask if the Israelites might go through his land, but the king refused. He was afraid they might hurt his people.

So the people went back to Mount Hor. There Aaron died, and his son Eleazar took his place as high priest.

About this time the King of Arad attacked the Israelites. The people begged the Lord to help them, and He did. They defeated the people of Arad, who were Canaanites.

Then the people marched back toward the Red Sea, discouraged and complaining again about food and water. So the Lord sent a plague of deadly snakes, and many people died

The Bronze Snake

from snakebite. "We have sinned," the people cried out to
Moses. "Pray for us."

So Moses prayed for the people.

"Make a bronze snake," the Lord ordered.
"Put it on a pole. When a snake bites
someone, the person should look at the
bronze snake. Then that person will
live."

Numbers 20:14–21:8

The Israelites asked permission to pass through the land of the Amorites, but their king refused. He attacked the Israelites, but the Lord helped His people defeat the Amorites. Next they defeated the King of Bashan, then they moved near Moab, across the Jordan River from Jericho.

The King of Moab sent for a false prophet named Balaam to curse the Israelites. But the Lord warned Balaam to say only what He told him, so Balaam blessed the Israelites instead. The Lord was using these experiences to prepare the Israelites to enter the Promised Land and fight for it.

One day the Lord told Moses that he would soon die on Mount Nebo. "You will look across the

Preparing to Enter the Promised Land

river at the Promised Land," He said. "Then you will die. You cannot go into the land because you disobeyed Me by hitting the rock instead of speaking to it."

Two of the tribes of Israel, those of Reuben and Gad, along with the half-tribe of Manasseh, had many sheep. Midian, the land the Israelites had just conquered, was great sheep country. So those tribes asked to stay there rather than go into the Promised Land. They promised first to go with the others to fight.

Then the Lord told Moses how to divide the Promised Land when they had conquered it, and gave him some more rules about offerings and feasts.

Numbers 25:1–36:13

At last it was time for Moses to die. He was 120 years old.

Moses called Joshua before the people and appointed him to take his place. Then Moses wrote out all the laws he had given to the people. He recited a great song to the people and blessed them.

Moses climbed onto Pisgah Peak on Mount Nebo. The Lord showed him the Promised Land across the Jordan River. There Moses died, and the Lord buried him.

"Moses is dead," the Lord then said to

The Israelites Enter Canaan, the Promised Land

Joshua. "You must lead My people across the Jordan River into the Promised Land. I will be with you, as I was with Moses. Be strong and brave. You and your people will conquer this land. But you must obey every one of My laws."

Joshua gave orders to the leaders of Israel to prepare their people to cross the Jordan River. "We will cross in three days," Joshua said. "We will conquer the land that God has given us."

Joshua reminded the tribes of Reuben, Gad, and the half-tribe of Manasseh of their promise to Moses. "You may live here east of the Jordan River. But your warriors must cross the Jordan with the rest of us and help us conquer the land."

They agreed with Joshua and promised to obey him.

1406 B.C.

Joshua 1; Deuteronomy 31:1–34:12

Joshua sent two spies across the Jordan River to look over the city of Jericho. They stayed with a woman named Rahab, but someone saw them.

The King of Jericho sent men to Rahab's house to demand that she turn the spies over to them.

"They were here earlier," she said, "but they left the city before the gates closed. Hurry! You may catch them." Actually Rahab had hidden the spies in piles of flax on her rooftop.

Before the men went to sleep, Rahab said, "Everyone is afraid of the Israelites. We have heard of the miracles the Lord has done for you and the victories you have had in battle. Promise me that when

Spies Visit Rahab

you conquer Jericho, you will let me and my family live because I helped you."

"Keep us safe, and we will keep you safe," the spies said. "Leave this red rope hanging from your window, and no one who stays in this house will be hurt. But if you betray us, we will not protect you."

So Rahab let the men down over the wall with the red rope, which she left hanging from her window.

"Hide in the mountains for three days," she said. "The people looking for you will come back by then."

So the spies did as Rahab said. Then they went back to Joshua and told him what they had seen.

"The Lord will give us the whole land," they said. "Everyone there is afraid of us."

*I*t was time to go into the Promised Land. When the Israelites got to the banks of the Jordan River, they camped for three days. "Tomorrow the Lord will work a great miracle," Joshua told them.

The next day he ordered the priests to carry the ark of the covenant to the river. "Listen to God!" Joshua called. "He will help you drive out your enemies."

When the priests who carried the ark touched the water with their feet, the river stopped flowing. All the people crossed on dry land. As the Lord had instructed him, Joshua ordered

The Israelites Cross the Jordan River

one man from each of the twelve tribes to take a stone from the middle of the river. The men built a monument from the stones.

"Now come out of the riverbed," Joshua commanded the priests, who were still standing there holding the ark. When they came out, the river began to flow again.

Joshua was looking toward Jericho when he saw a man with his sword drawn. "Are You a friend or an enemy?" Joshua asked.

"I am the Commander of the Lord's army," the man said.

Joshua bowed down before him. "What do You want?" Joshua asked. "Take off your shoes," the man said. "This is holy ground." So Joshua took off his shoes and worshiped the Lord's Commander.

Joshua 3:1–5:15

The people of Jericho shut their gates because they were afraid. But the Lord said, "I have already given you the victory. Walk around the city each day for six days. The priests will follow, carrying the ark. On the seventh day, walk around Jericho seven times, with the priests blowing on rams' horns. At the end they will give one long, loud blast, and everyone must shout! The walls of Jericho will fall down."

That is exactly what happened. The Israelites defeated Jericho completely, sparing only Rahab and her family.

The Lord said they were not to take loot from Jericho, but Achan disobeyed. So when Israelite soldiers went to battle against Ai, they were defeated.

Conquering the Promised Land

When Joshua asked the Lord why, He answered, "There is sin in your camp." Achan confessed and was quickly executed. "Now you will defeat Ai," the Lord said. And they did.

One day some Gibeonites came and tricked Joshua into making a peace treaty. When Joshua learned that they were really enemies trying to save themselves, he made them servants of Israel for the rest of their lives.

Another time the King of Jerusalem gathered four other kings to fight Gibeon, the city that had tricked Joshua into a peace treaty. Now Joshua had to defend them. His army traveled all night and attacked the five enemy kings. Suddenly a hailstorm pounded down on these kings. Then Joshua cried out, "Let the sun and moon stand still," because he needed more daylight to conquer the enemies. So the sun stopped for almost twenty-four hours.

Later Joshua defeated many other kings of the land. The rest of the Book of Joshua tells how he divided the land among his people.

Joshua 6–11

Before Joshua died he reminded the Israelites to be faithful to the Lord. But when the people settled down in the Promised Land, the generation that conquered the land died off. A new generation grew up and they forgot the Lord. They disobeyed His laws and even worshiped foreign idols.

The new rulers of Israel were called judges. Most of them were not strong, godly people like Moses and Joshua. This was a troubled time for Israel. Often they were defeated in battle. At times their enemies ruled over them.

One judge was a woman named Deborah. She was a godly woman and a strong person.

Deborah

Deborah becomes a judge 1209 B.C.

One time the Israelites came to Deborah for help. She asked Barak to go to war with her. He gathered 10,000 warriors of Israel and defeated General Sisera and his Canaanite army.

But the Israelites began to worship foreign idols again. As they did, they grew weaker. So the cruel Midianites made life miserable for them.

1200 B.C. Iron Age begins

Judges 4:1–6:10

One day the Angel of the Lord sat under an oak tree talking with Gideon, who was threshing wheat near-by. "Go and save Israel," the angel said. The Angel was really the Lord.

Gideon asked the Angel for a miracle to show that this was really God calling him to fight.

Gideon put some wool on the ground. "If You are calling me to help You, make the wool wet while the ground is dry," said Gideon. The next morning the wool was wet and the ground was dry.

Gideon

1162 B.C. Gideon becomes a judge

The next night Gideon asked the Lord to keep the wool dry while the ground was wet. That is what happened.

So Gideon gathered a great army. "There are too many," the Lord said. "Send away those who are afraid." So 22,000 warriors went home.

"There are still too many," the Lord said. "Go to the spring. Keep only those who use their hands to drink." Only 300 men did that.

Gideon gave each warrior a torch and jug. That night they covered the torches with the jugs and surrounded the enemy camp. Just after midnight they blew on their trumpets. They broke the jugs, and lights shone around the camp. The enemy ran away in fear. But Gideon and his warriors chased the Midianites and defeated them.

Judges 6:11–7:25

One day the Angel of the Lord appeared to Manoah's wife. "You will have a son who will rescue Israel from the Philistines," he said.

She ran to tell her husband. Then Manoah asked the Angel how they should raise this baby.

When the baby was born they named him Samson. He became a very strong man, but sometimes he made very foolish choices.

When Samson grew up he wanted to marry a Philistine girl. Of course his father and mother were sad. "Marry an Israelite girl," they begged. "No," said Samson. "I want this girl."

But on the way to meet her, Samson was attacked by a lion.

In the Time of the Judges: Samson

He grabbed the lion and tore it apart. That's how strong he was!

Not long after his wedding to the Philistine girl, Samson became angry with his bride and left her. So her parents let her marry someone else.

Samson was furious when he heard this. He and the Philistines kept trying to hurt each other.

But as Samson would learn, that always makes things worse. When a person doesn't do things God's way, everything seems to go from bad to worse. Samson had great strength, but he didn't use it the way God wanted him to use it.

Judges 13:1–14:20

Samson was the leader of
Israel and the strongest man alive.
But even he couldn't seem to do
things God's way.

Samson was angry with the Philistines, so he
tied torches between the tails of some foxes
and set them loose to burn the fields. Then
the Philistines tried to hurt Samson. Then he
tried to hurt them. So it went.

Samson fell in love with another Philistine
woman, Delilah. He told her the secret of his
great strength: If anyone cut his hair, he
would be no stronger than an ordinary man.

Delilah sold this secret to some
Philistines, who

Samson Gets into Big Trouble

then captured Samson and blinded him.

The Philistines celebrated Samson's defeat. They brought Samson to their great temple and made fun of him.

Then Samson talked to the little boy who had led him there. "Put my hands against those two big pillars," he said. "I want to rest." When the boy did that, Samson pushed with all his might against the pillars, and the temple came crashing down, killing thousands of Philistines and Samson himself.

Samson's story is sad. He could have led his nation God's way, but he made terrible choices and died with his enemies.

So it was through the times of the judges. They did not often work hard for the good of their neighbors or nation. It was a dismal time in the history of Israel.

Judges 15:1–16:31

During the time of the judges, there was a famine in Israel. Elimelech and Naomi moved from Bethlehem to the foreign land of Moab. Elimelech died there, but his sons Mahlon and Chilion grew up and married Moabite women. Then Mahlon and Chilion died. Now Naomi was alone in Moab with her two daughters-in-law.

Naomi heard that there was now food in Israel, so she and her daughters-in-law set out for the land of Judah. But Naomi changed her mind. "Please go home to your families," she said. She kissed them, and they all cried.

One daughter-in-law, Orpah, went home. But Ruth would not go. "I won't leave you," she said. "I will go where you go. Your God will be my God. Your people will be my people."

The Story of Ruth

So Naomi and Ruth went to Bethlehem. Naomi was too old to work, so Ruth worked in the fields for both of them, gathering grain that the reapers left behind. The owner of one field, Boaz, was related to Naomi. In time Ruth met Boaz. Before long they married.

Boaz and Ruth had a baby boy, Obed, Naomi's grandson. He became the father of Jesse and the grandfather of King David. Much, much later the names of Boaz, Ruth, Obed, Jesse, and King David appeared in the family tree of Jesus.★ So remember this beautiful story from a very sad time. It was important in the Greatest Story Ever Told, the story of Jesus.

★See Matthew 1:5-6.

The Book of Ruth

An Israelite named Elkanah had two wives, Peninnah and Hannah. (In those days men could have more than one wife, but it often brought trouble to a family.)

Peninnah had children, but Hannah did not. So Peninnah made fun of Hannah, and Hannah was very sad.

Each year Elkanah and his family went from their home to visit the tabernacle at Shiloh. There Hannah prayed, "Lord, if You give me a son, I will give him back to You."★

One time Eli, the high priest, saw her. At first he thought she was drunk, but when he realized she was praying, he blessed her. "May the Lord give you what you want," he said.

In time, Hannah had a baby boy. "As soon as he is old enough, I will leave him in God's service at the tabernacle," she said.

Samuel Is Born and Given to God
1105 B.C.

When Samuel was still a little boy, Elkanah and Hannah took the child to Eli. "I prayed here that the Lord would give me this child," Hannah told him. "Now I am giving him to the Lord. He will help you do the Lord's work."

It must have been very sad for Hannah to give up the son that she had wanted so much. But it also must have made her happy that Samuel would be a special young man. He would become the last judge of Israel and serve the Lord all his life.

★ Read Hannah's prayer in 1 Samuel 2.

1 Samuel 1

As Samuel grew, life at the tabernacle was not easy for him. He saw how evil Eli's grown sons were. They did not honor the Lord. They did many sinful things, even in God's house. "The Lord will punish you," Eli told them, but they wouldn't listen.

One day a prophet came to the tabernacle and gave Eli a message from the Lord. "Your sons will not live long," he warned. "They will not do your work when you are gone."

One night Samuel was sleeping near the ark, the box that held the Ten Commandments. Suddenly a voice called his name. Samuel thought it was Eli. He ran to ask what Eli wanted.

"I didn't call you," Eli said. This happened three times. Then Eli knew that the Lord was talking to Samuel. "Go back to bed," he told Samuel. "When the Lord calls, tell Him you are listening."

God Speaks to the Boy Samuel

When Samuel did, the Lord told him that He would punish Eli and his family. They would not carry on His work.

In the morning Samuel was afraid to tell Eli what the Lord had said, but Eli insisted.

When he heard the message, Eli said, "It is the Lord's will. Let Him do what is best."

As Samuel grew up, the Lord was with him. The Israelites knew that he would be God's prophet. They listened to Samuel, for they knew that the Lord spoke through him.

1 Samuel 2:12–3:21

*I*srael and the Philistines were at war. In one battle, the Philistines killed 4,000 Israelites.

"What can we do?" the Israelite leaders asked. "Let's bring God's ark into battle with us," said others. "Then the Lord will be with us."

So they carried the ark, the golden chest holding the Ten Commandments, into battle. Eli's sons Hophni and Phinehas went with it.

At first the Philistines were afraid. They had heard how the Lord had helped Israel through the years. So they fought harder than ever, and they won. The Philistines killed 30,000 Israelites, including Hophni and Phinehas. They even captured the ark and took it home with them.

The Ark Is Captured and Returned

When ninety-eight-year-old Eli heard this news, he fell over, broke his neck, and died.

The Philistines put the ark in the temple of their idol Dagon. That night the great statue of Dagon fell on its face. The next night it happened again, breaking off the idol's head and hands. Then the Philistines began dying of a plague. They knew what was wrong.

"We can't keep the ark," they said, "or we will all die." So they decided to return it to Israel.

The Philistines put the ark on a new cart. They hitched two cows that had just had calves to the cart and turned them loose. "If the cows go back to their calves, we will know the Lord isn't guiding them," they said. "But if they don't, we will know the Lord is doing this." The cows went straight for Israel, mooing all the way.

1 Samuel 4:1–6:12

*W*hen the ark came back to Israel, the people put it in the home of Eleazar at a town called Kiriath Jearim. There it stayed for the next twenty years.

But the people of Israel were sad. They were afraid to move the ark to the tabernacle, where it should be, because when seventy men had looked inside the box, they all died.

"If you really want to move the ark back to the tabernacle, get rid of your idols and obey the Lord," Samuel said. So that's what they did. Samuel brought the people together at Mizpah.

Saul Becomes King

1050 B.C.

They fasted and prayed and told the Lord how sorry they were for their sins.

The Philistines heard about this meeting and thought it was a good time to attack the Israelites. "Beg God to save us!" the Israelites said to Samuel. When Samuel did that, the Lord sent thunder and confused the Philistines. Then Israel defeated them. For a long time, the Philistines left the Israelites alone.

For the rest of his life, Samuel was judge over Israel. When he grew old, he retired and put his sons in his place, but they were greedy and took bribes. The Israelites thought it was time for a king, as other nations had.

Samuel warned the people about the trouble they would have, but they insisted. So the Lord arranged for Samuel to make Saul the first King of Israel.

1 Samuel 7:1–12:25

Saul was a big man with a great future. The Lord had chosen him and Samuel had anointed him. But so far he had not done any kingly thing.

One day King Nahash led his Ammonite army against a city of Israel. The people of the city sent word to Saul.

Saul killed his oxen and sent pieces throughout Israel. "If you don't join my army, I'll do this to your oxen," he warned. Saul had an army quickly! They attacked the Ammonites and defeated them.

"Come to Gilgal," Samuel said. There before the Lord the people made offerings and crowned Saul king. Samuel told the people, "If you and your king

King Saul's Big Mistakes

trust in the Lord and obey Him, all will be well."

When Saul had been king a year, he and his son Jonathan went to war with the Philistines. Saul called out the whole army of Israel while the Philistines gathered even more chariots and horsemen. Now the Israelite warriors were afraid. Many ran away and hid.

King Saul grew nervous. Samuel had said he would make an offering to the Lord, but he hadn't come yet. So Saul made the offering himself. He was just finishing when Samuel walked up.

"You have disobeyed the Lord," Samuel said. "The Lord wants a king who will obey Him. He had planned to make you and your descendants kings for a long, long time. Now someone else will become king instead of you."

1 Samuel 11:1–13:14

Things looked bad. King Saul had only 600 warriors left. He had foolishly made an offering that God's prophet should have made. Not only that, but the Philistines knew how to make iron weapons and the Israelites did not. Only Saul and Jonathan had swords.

Jonathan said to his bodyguard, "Let's go to the Philistine camp. Perhaps the Lord will work a miracle for us." But he didn't tell his father. Jonathan and his bodyguard attacked the Philistines and killed about twenty of them. Suddenly the Philistines were afraid. Then an earthquake came, and the Philistines began killing each other.

Saul called for the ark of God. Then he and his 600 men rushed into the battle. The Israelites who had deserted joined the battle. "A curse on anyone who eats before evening," Saul declared.

Jonathan Shows How Brave He Is

But Jonathan had not heard this, so he ate some honey to give him strength. That night Saul wanted to keep fighting the Philistines, but the Lord would not answer when he prayed. "Something is wrong," Saul said. Then the truth came out. "Jonathan must die!" Saul said.

But the warriors would not let that happen. "Jonathan saved us today," they said. So Saul stopped going after the Philistines. The Philistines were tired of fighting, so they went home.

Saul had made a foolish promise to God. Now Israel was hurt by it. So don't make promises to the Lord unless you know that you will keep them.

1 Samuel 13:16–14:52

Now King Saul was given another opportunity to obey the Lord completely. "Obey the Lord!" Samuel said. "He wants you to punish the nation of Amalek because they wouldn't let the Israelites cross their land on the way to the Promised Land. Go, destroy the whole nation. Nothing must survive."

Saul gathered his army and went to war against the Amalekites. Then Saul captured King Agag and some of the best sheep and oxen, even though the Lord said that nothing should survive.

"I'm sorry I made Saul king," the Lord told Samuel. Samuel cried all night when he heard that. Then he went to find Saul. "I've done my job," Saul said.

Samuel Anoints David as the New King

"Then what is the sound of animals that I hear?" Samuel answered. Saul tried to make excuses. Then he cried out, "I have sinned."

"Yes," said Samuel. "And God has chosen another king."

So the Lord sent Samuel to Bethlehem to anoint one of Jesse's sons. One by one, Jesse brought his sons to Samuel. But not one of them was the Lord's choice. "Do you have any more sons?" Samuel asked. "Yes, the youngest is taking care of the sheep," Jesse answered.

"Bring him here," Samuel said. When they did, the Lord said, "This is the one!" While the older brothers watched, Samuel anointed David to become the next king someday.

1 Samuel 15:1–16:13

Saul had made many foolish choices, so the Lord was no longer with him. Instead, Saul was a troubled man. "We'll find a good harp player," some of Saul's helpers said. "He will play for you when you are troubled." Saul thought that was a good idea.

One of Saul's helpers remembered that David was an excellent harp player. "Not only that, but he's a good-looking young man and the Lord is with him."

So Saul sent messengers to Jesse, and Jesse sent David to play for King Saul. He also sent

David Plays for King Saul

a gift of a young goat and a donkey with a load of food and wine.

Saul liked David immediately. "Please let David join my staff," Saul said to Jesse. So that is what happened.

David even became King Saul's bodyguard. Whenever Saul was troubled, David played his harp for him. That helped Saul feel better.

Time passed. David went back and forth between his work for Saul and his shepherd work for his father.

1 Samuel 16:14-23

*T*he Philistines went to war against Israel.

Goliath, a nine-foot giant, challenged the Israelites. Every morning and every evening for forty days he came out and shouted, "Send a man to fight me! If I kill him, you will be our slaves. If he kills me, we will be your slaves."

Saul promised that the person who defeated Goliath could marry his daughter, but the Israelite warriors were terrified. No one would fight him.

David Fights Goliath

When David heard about Goliath, he talked with King Saul. "I'll fight this giant," he said. "Don't be foolish," Saul answered. "He's a giant and you're only a boy."

"But I have fought lions and bears," David said.

No one else was brave enough to fight Goliath, so finally Saul agreed. David picked up five smooth stones and went out to face the warrior. Goliath was insulted and cursed David.

"You come to me with great weapons," David shouted, "but I have the Lord on my side." He put a stone in his sling and whirled it around and around. Then he sent the stone flying straight for Goliath's forehead. The stone sank into the giant's head, and Goliath fell to the ground. Then David pulled out Goliath's own sword and cut off his head.

1 Samuel 17

Though the bravest soldiers of Israel would not go out to fight Goliath, David fought him with only a shepherd's rod and a sling. The Lord was with him because David had asked Him to be there. So David, whom King Saul called "only a boy," won the battle. This gave the whole Israelite army the courage to chase the Philistines and win.

David and Jonathan Become Friends

Prince Jonathan, King Saul's son, watched all this. He was a very brave young man too. He had helped his father win another battle against the Philistines. He also trusted the Lord to help him.

Jonathan saw how brave David was and how he trusted the Lord. He wanted David to be his best friend. After the battle Jonathan promised to be David's blood brother, just as if the two of them had been born into the same family.

To seal this promise, Prince Jonathan gave David his robe, sword, bow, and belt. So that day David and Jonathan became close friends. Their friendship lasted as long as they both were alive.

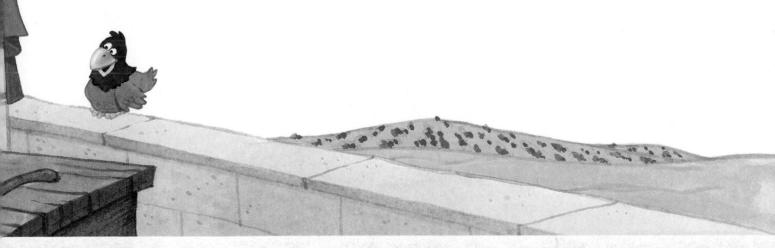

1 Samuel 18:1-4

King Saul made David commander of his entire army. As they went toward his royal home, women came along the way to sing to them, but they sang greater praises to David. This made Saul angry and jealous. But he had promised that the person who defeated Goliath would marry his daughter. Saul's youngest daughter, Michal, fell in love with David, so before long Saul said they could get married.

David was successful in everything he did, because the Lord was with him. This only made Saul more jealous, and several times he tried to kill David. Twice when David was playing soothing harp music to Saul, the king threw his spear at David.

Finally Michal helped David run away. Saul sent soldiers to capture him, but David hid.

"Why does your father want to kill me?" David asked Jonathan. At first Jonathan didn't believe it, but then Saul tried to kill him when he said good things about David.

Saul Is Jealous of David

One day David and his men were hiding in a cave. It happened that Saul went into that same cave for a few minutes. His men urged David to kill him, but he wouldn't because Saul was the king. When Saul left the cave David shouted to him. "I could have killed you in there, but I didn't!"

Saul was ashamed and went home. David was safe for a while.

1 Samuel 18:5–24:22

When the Prophet Samuel died, he was buried at a place called Ramah. David was still running away from King Saul. One day he came near the home of a wealthy man named Nabal. David sent ten of his men to ask Nabal for some food, but Nabal sneered at David and made fun of him. He would not give him food for himself and his men.

Even though Nabal was a rude person, he had a lovely wife named Abigail. She heard what had happened and put a lot of food on donkeys, which she took to David and his men.

Abigail Stops a Fight

She was just in time, for they were preparing to attack Nabal. Abigail was very gracious to David. "Bless the Lord," David told her. "He has sent you. You are certainly a sensible person." He took Abigail's gifts, and she went home.

At home Abigail found Nabal drunk at a big party, so she did not tell him what she had done until the next morning. Nabal was so angry that he had a stroke, and ten days later he died. Then David sent messengers to Abigail and asked her to marry him. She agreed and brought five servant girls to help with her work.

1 Samuel 25:1-44

Saul and his soldiers were still chasing David. One night Saul set up camp at the edge of the wilderness where David was hiding. Saul and General Abner went to sleep inside a circle of sleeping soldiers.

"Anyone want to sneak into Saul's camp with me?" David asked.

"I'll go," Abishai answered.

So the two of them slipped into Saul's camp and sneaked right up to the king.

"Let me kill him," Abishai whispered.

"No," David answered. "We can't attack the Lord's chosen king."

David Visits Saul's Camp at Night

He took Saul's spear and water jug, then the two of them slipped away without waking anyone.

The next morning David shouted, "Wake up, Abner! You're a great guard. Look what I took last night!" He continued, "Why are you hunting me like this? What have I done?"

Now King Saul was awake too, and he saw that David could have killed him.

"I have sinned," Saul said. "Come home. I won't hurt you."

But David knew that Saul would still try to hurt him, so he decided to live with the Philistines. He pretended to go on raiding parties against his own people, but instead he raided other people on the road to Egypt.

The Philistine king Achish mistakenly thought the Israelites would hate David and that David would have to serve him from now on.

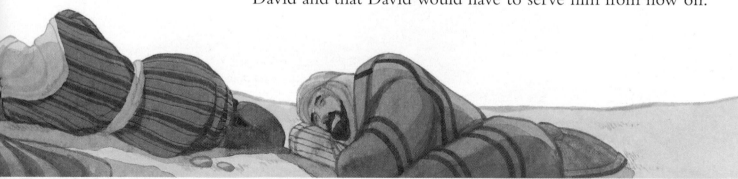

1 Samuel 26:1–27:12

About this time the Philistines planned another war against Israel. When Saul saw their great army he was afraid and asked the Lord for help. But the Lord would not answer him.

Then Saul dressed in common clothes and went to Endor to see a witch. He asked her to call Samuel from the dead.

She was afraid. "You know that King Saul is killing all the witches," she said. But she went ahead and called for Samuel.

Samuel appeared and asked, "What do you want?"

Saul Is Killed in Battle

"I'm in trouble," Saul said. "I need your help."

But Samuel told him that his whole army would be defeated the next day, and Saul and his sons would die.

Meanwhile, King Achish had asked David to fight with him against the Israelites, but the Philistine commanders did not like this. They thought David and his men would turn against them in battle. So David's men returned to their home at Ziklag, where they found that Amalekites had raided the town and captured their wives and children.

The Lord told David to chase the Amalekites. David and his men defeated the Amalekites and took back their wives and children and possessions.

The Philistines, meanwhile, fought the Israelite army, led by King Saul. The Philistines killed Saul, Jonathan, Saul's bodyguard, and Saul's other two sons. It was a very sad day for Israel.

1 Samuel 28:1–31:13

A man from the Israelite army, ragged and dirty, came to David. "Our army was defeated," he said. "Thousands died, including Saul and Jonathan."

David and his people cried all day when they heard this terrible news. Then David wrote a beautiful funeral song for Saul and Jonathan.★

The Lord told David to go to Hebron, where the leaders of Judah crowned him king. But the rest of Israel crowned Saul's son Ish-Bosheth king.

★The song is found in 2 Samuel 1:17-27.

David Becomes King

1010 B.C.

For two years the Israelites were divided, with two kings and two armies fighting each other.

One day Ish-Bosheth accused Abner, David's general, of something. This made Abner angry. He made a deal with David: He would help David become king of all Israel if David would then make him general of the whole Israelite army. Joab, the other general, was angry when he heard about this, so he murdered Abner. Then two other men murdered Ish-Bosheth.

Now the leaders of all the tribes of Israel made David their king. They crowned him at Hebron when he was only thirty years old. David led his army against Jerusalem and captured it. He made Jerusalem his capital and built a beautiful palace there. He brought the ark back to Jerusalem too.

David was king of Judah for seven years, then he was king in Jerusalem for thirty-three years. So altogether he reigned for forty years.

2 Samuel 1:1–5:25

At last all of the tribes of Israel were united with David as their king. Jerusalem was their beautiful capital city. The nation of Israel was stronger than any of the other nations around.

One day David called Nathan the prophet to him. "Here I am living in this beautiful cedar palace," he said, "while the ark of God is in a tent." David wanted to build a beautiful temple for the Lord.

But the Lord spoke to Nathan. "Tell David not to build a temple," He said. "Tell him I will make his family great as long as they obey Me. David's kingdom shall be for all time."

David Plans for the Temple

David went into the tabernacle, God's tent house that the Israelites had carried through the wilderness and was now set up in Jerusalem. "Oh Lord," he prayed. "Who am I that You should do such great things to me? Help my family rule for a long time." Then David worshiped the Lord for all that He had done.

Some of the heathen nations around David would not fight him. They kept him from hurting them by paying taxes each year. But David had to fight other nations. He conquered them and made them pay taxes.

David now had a lot of gold and silver, but he gave it to the Lord. He became a great king and a powerful military leader, rich and famous. But he ruled Israel well. He was fair and just.

2 Samuel 7

One day David was thinking about Saul's family. He had promised Jonathan that he would be kind to his relatives. So David called for Ziba, one of Saul's servants. "Are any of Saul's family still alive?" he asked.

"Yes," Ziba answered. "Jonathan's son, Mephibosheth, is alive."

Mephibosheth was lame in both feet, because his nurse had accidentally dropped him when he was a baby.

Mephibosheth was terrified when he came before David. He thought David would kill him. But David told him about his promise to Jonathan. He wanted to show kindness to him.

David Is Kind to Mephibosheth

"You will live here at the palace with me," David said. "You will eat at my table. I will also give you the farms that belonged to King Saul."

Then David talked to Ziba. "You were King Saul's servant," he said. "Now you and your family will serve Mephibosheth. You will farm his land and take care of his family."

So Ziba and his family served Mephibosheth, the lame prince. Mephibosheth moved into David's palace and ate at his table. David treated him as if he were his own son.

2 Samuel 9

*E*verything was going well for David and his people. That is always a time to be careful, isn't it? When we have too much, we may be tempted to get into trouble.

One of David's troubles came from the Ammonites. When their king died, his son became king. David sent some men to make peace with him. But he cut off their robes at the hips and shaved their beards down the middle. He sent them home ashamed.

Then the Ammonites realized they had made David their enemy. So they went to war against him. David sent General Joab to finish the war against the Ammonites.

King David's Troubles

While this was happening, David got into trouble with a beautiful lady named Bathsheba. Her husband was away, helping Joab fight the Ammonites. David wanted her to be his wife, so he arranged to have her husband killed. It was a very sad time in David's life. In the end, David married Bathsheba. She became the mother of Solomon, Israel's next king.

David's next trouble came from his own sons. David's son Amnon hurt the sister of David's son Absalom. So Absalom murdered Amnon.

Then Absalom rebelled against King David and tried to become king himself. Some people followed Absalom and some followed David. Again, it was a very sad time in Israel.

Finally David had to run for his life. Absalom and his warriors went after David to kill him.

2 Samuel 10:1–17:29

Finally, David's men defeated the army of Israel. In this battle Absalom met David's men. As he was riding his mule under a tree, his hair caught in the branches while his mule kept going. When Joab heard that Absalom was hanging in the tree, he killed him. The rebellion was over. But it had brought much sadness and hurt to Israel. David mourned greatly for Absalom, even though his son had tried to kill him.

After Absalom's death, David returned to Jerusalem. But the people of Judah and the people of the other tribes of Israel quarreled over who should get the honor for bringing David home.

One day a man named Sheba rebelled against David. Many people followed him instead of David. General Joab led the attack and before long, Sheba's rebellion was put down.

Then a famine came to the land. It lasted for three years. David prayed and decided

David Is King Again But He Still Has Troubles

that the famine was punishment for some terrible things King Saul had done to the people of Gibeon. David talked with the Gibeonites. "What should I do?" he asked.

"Give us King Saul's seven sons," they said. "We will execute them."

When that was done, the famine stopped. Then King David wrote a beautiful song of praise to the Lord.★

★See 2 Samuel 22.

2 Samuel 18:1–22:5

Once when things were going well for King David, he got the idea of counting his fighting men. So he ordered General Joab to count the warriors.

Joab warned David not to do it. "You have no right to do this just to feel good," he said.

But David was king, so he ordered Joab to do it anyway. It took more than nine months to count the 800,000 men of fighting age in Israel and 500,000 in Judah.

After this was done, David began to worry. Then he confessed his sin to the Lord. "It was wrong for me to do this," he said. "Please forgive me."

The Lord sent a message to David. "You have three choices. You can have famine for seven years. Or you can run from your enemies for three months. Or you will have three days of plague."

David Buys a Threshing Floor

"This is hard," David said. "But I would rather have the Lord punish us than our enemies."
So he chose the plague. During the next three days, 70,000 people died. The death angel
stood at Araunah's threshing floor pointing his sword toward Jerusalem to destroy it.

"Stop punishing the people," David begged. "I am the one who sinned. Punish me."

The Lord told David to build an altar there
and give offerings to the Lord.

2 Samuel 24; 1 Chronicles 21

W hen the great plague stopped and David had built the altar there on the mountaintop above Jerusalem, he said, "This is the place where we must build the temple for the Lord."

Long before, David had talked with the Lord about this. He wanted to build it, but the Lord said no, he must let his son Solomon build it. "You are a warrior," the Lord had told David. "You have killed too many people in battles. Solomon will be a man of peace, so he will build the temple."

David and Solomon Plan the Temple

But it was time to start preparing to build, and David could do that. He cut great blocks of stone and made many iron nails that would be used for the doors, gates, and clamps. He melted bronze. He brought great cedar logs from Tyre and Sidon. The gold alone was worth several billion dollars.

David spent his last years gathering these building materials. He gathered skilled workmen to do the job. He gave the priests and Levites special instructions about their work in the temple. He appointed musicians and temple guards. He also helped to organize the army that would serve under Solomon.

By now David was an old man. He gave Solomon orders to build the temple and chose him as the new king to rule in his palace.

1 Chronicles 22-27

David had chosen Solomon as king, but had not yet turned over the kingdom. Then one day David's son Adonijah proclaimed himself king. He gathered many important people, including David's other sons.

The Prophet Nathan went quickly to Solomon's mother, Bathsheba. "You must do something," he warned. "Remind David that he promised that Solomon would be king."

So Bathsheba and Nathan went to talk with David, who was quite old and in bed.

"Take Solomon to Gihon spring and anoint him as king," David commanded. "Then bring him back here and put him on my throne."

Solomon Becomes King

970 B.C.

When this happened, there was a great celebration with much noise.

When Adonijah heard that David had made Solomon king, he was frightened. He ran into the tabernacle and held onto the horns of the altar. (This was a "safe place"—people were not supposed to be killed when they held onto those horns.)

David called all the important leaders to Jerusalem. The leaders gave gold and silver, bronze and iron. David gave Solomon the written plans for the temple and challenged him to be a good king and faithful to the Lord. Once more the people crowned Solomon as their king. There was a big celebration.

David had ruled for forty years and was Israel's greatest king. Before he died, he told Solomon again that he must obey the Lord.

1 Kings 1; 1 Chronicles 28–29

One night the Lord spoke to Solomon in a dream. "Ask whatever you wish, and I will give it to you."

"Give me wisdom to rule my people well," Solomon answered.

This pleased the Lord. "You did not ask for selfish things, such as riches or long life or victory over your enemies. So I will give you all of these plus wisdom! I will make you the wisest person who ever lived."

Soon after that two women came to Solomon with a problem. "We both had babies," one woman said. "Her baby died when she rolled over on it at night. She stole mine to take its place and put the dead baby beside me." But the other woman said the living baby was hers.

Solomon Asks for Wisdom

959 B.C. Temple built

"Bring me a sword," said Solomon. "I will cut the baby in two and give each of you half."

"No!" cried the first mother. "Let her have it."

So Solomon knew she was the real mother and gave the baby to her. Now the people knew how wise Solomon really was.

The time came to build the temple for the Lord. Solomon had 180,000 people working on it. When it was done, the ark was brought to Jerusalem and put into the temple. Solomon held a great dedication ceremony that lasted for fourteen days. He prayed and praised the Lord before all the people. Together they dedicated this beautiful building to the Lord.

1 Kings 3:1–9:28

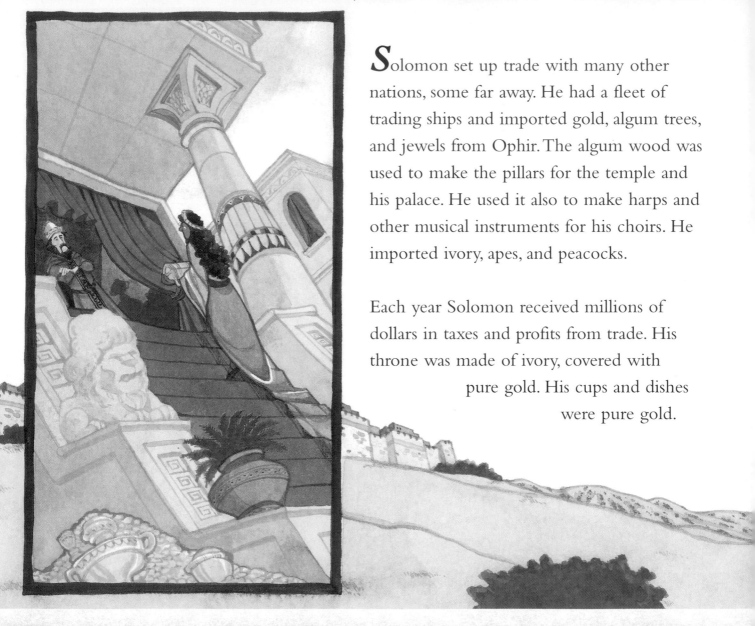

Solomon set up trade with many other nations, some far away. He had a fleet of trading ships and imported gold, algum trees, and jewels from Ophir. The algum wood was used to make the pillars for the temple and his palace. He used it also to make harps and other musical instruments for his choirs. He imported ivory, apes, and peacocks.

Each year Solomon received millions of dollars in taxes and profits from trade. His throne was made of ivory, covered with pure gold. His cups and dishes were pure gold.

The Queen of Sheba Visits Solomon

He had stables for his horses, which came from Egypt and southern Turkey. He had chariots and horsemen.

Solomon's fame spread to other nations. The Queen of Sheba heard about his riches and wisdom and came to see him. She brought rich gifts and asked Solomon many questions, all of which he answered wisely. She saw all his beautiful buildings and treasures.

"I didn't believe it before, but all that I have heard is true," she said.

Solomon gave her beautiful gifts too, as much as she had given him. At last the queen went home with her servants.

Solomon was the wisest king alive. He was also the richest king in the world. As long as he obeyed the Lord, the Lord was with him.

1 Kings 10; 2 Chronicles 9:1-28

Solomon was the wisest and richest man alive. He had everything. But when we have everything, it is time to be careful. We may have too much and forget about the Lord. That's what happened to Solomon.

To keep peace, Solomon did not go to war as his father David had done. He married the daughters of neighboring kings. The kings would not go to war against their son-in-law.

Solomon had 700 wives and 300 concubines. (Concubines were women who were treated like wives, but the king owned them. They didn't have as much freedom as wives.) But these foreign

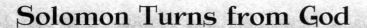

Solomon Turns from God

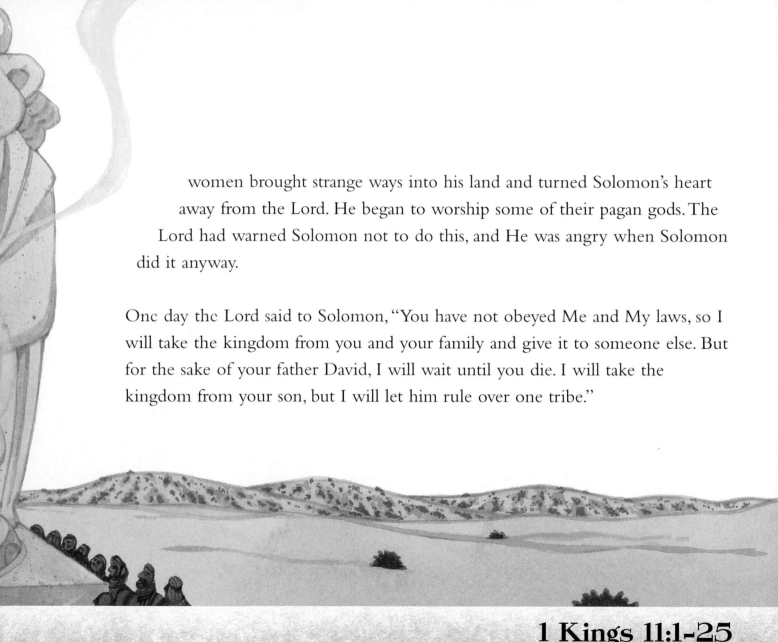

women brought strange ways into his land and turned Solomon's heart away from the Lord. He began to worship some of their pagan gods. The Lord had warned Solomon not to do this, and He was angry when Solomon did it anyway.

One day the Lord said to Solomon, "You have not obeyed Me and My laws, so I will take the kingdom from you and your family and give it to someone else. But for the sake of your father David, I will wait until you die. I will take the kingdom from your son, but I will let him rule over one tribe."

1 Kings 11:1-25

During King Solomon's reign, a man named
Jeroboam was in charge of some labor groups in Israel.
He was a very capable man.

One day the Prophet Ahijah met Jeroboam along a road. Ahijah took
his new cloak and tore it into twelve parts, then he gave ten of them to
Jeroboam.

"The Lord will give you ten tribes of Israel to rule," Ahijah said.
"Solomon has turned from Him to worship foreign gods.
But the Lord will let him keep one tribe for the sake
of his father, King David. When he dies, his son may
also rule that tribe."

Solomon must have heard about this, for he tried

The Kingdom Divides

930 B.C.

to kill Jeroboam. But Jeroboam ran away to Egypt and stayed there until Solomon died.

Solomon's son Rehoboam became king, and Jeroboam came home from Egypt.

Although Rehoboam's older counselors said he should be kind to Jeroboam's people, he listened to his younger counselors, who said he should be harsher. So the people rebelled, and all except the tribe of Judah left him.

Many people still went to Jerusalem in Judah (Rehoboam's territory), to worship. Jeroboam was afraid this would make them turn back to Rehoboam. So he made two golden calves for the people to worship in their own kingdom.

This was a terrible thing for Jeroboam to do. A prophet warned him that he had turned away from the Lord, but Jeroboam would not listen to him.

1 Kings 11:26–13:10; 2 Chronicles 9:29–11:4

This is what happened to the kings of Israel. Jeroboam ruled Israel, the ten tribes, for twenty-two years. When he died, his son Nadab ruled. Then Baasha rebelled against Nadab, and ruled in his place.

Baasha was an evil man who did not please the Lord. Later Baasha's son became ruler of Israel, but for only two years. General Zimri killed him and became ruler of Israel.

General Zimri lasted only seven days. Then the army put General Omri in his place. Omri was the worst King of Israel yet. When he died, Ahab took his

Troubled Times for a Divided Nation

place. Ahab married Jezebel, a very wicked foreign princess, and became an even worse king than Omri.

Meanwhile, this is what happened to the kings of Judah. Rehoboam ruled Judah for seventeen years. During his rule, King Shishak conquered Jerusalem and took all of the gold back to Egypt.

When Rehoboam died, his son Abijam ruled Judah, but he was just as evil as his father. When he died Asa became ruler. Asa was a good king, as David had been. He went to war against Israel when Baasha was King of Israel. It was a very sad time for Israel and Judah.

Elijah was a prophet during the time of King Ahab of Israel. One day he went to Ahab with a warning. "There will be no rain for several years." Then he hid by Cherith Brook, as the Lord told him to do. He drank from the brook. Ravens brought him food.

As Elijah had said, there was no rain in Israel. Eventually even the brook went dry. The Lord told Elijah to go to the city of Zarephath, where a widow would feed him. Elijah found her gathering sticks. He asked her for some bread and water.

"I have only a handful of flour and a little cooking oil," she said. "I was just ready to bake the last meal for my son and me."

"Bake a little loaf of bread for me," Elijah said. "After that you will always have flour and oil until the rains come and crops grow again."

Elijah Helps a Widow at Zarephath

The woman obeyed Elijah. From that time on she always had flour and cooking oil.

One day the widow's son became sick and died. She begged Elijah for help. Elijah in turn begged the Lord for help. Then he spread himself upon the child three times and prayed. The Lord heard Elijah's prayers and brought the boy back to life. Elijah brought the boy to his mother.

"You truly are a prophet," the woman said. "I know that what you say comes from the Lord."

*F*or three years there had been a famine in Israel. One day the Lord told Elijah to go back to King Ahab. "Tell him that it will rain soon," the Lord said. So Elijah sent a message to the king through the king's godly servant Obadiah.

"Bring the people of Israel to Mount Carmel," Elijah instructed. "Bring all 450 prophets of Baal there too, as well as 400 prophets of Asherah."

King Ahab hated Elijah and had looked everywhere for him, hoping to kill him. But he listened to Obadiah's message.

Elijah Defeats the Prophets of Baal

When the people gathered, Elijah called out to them. "If the Lord is God, serve Him," he said. "But if Baal is God, then follow him."

Then Elijah had the prophets of Baal cut up a young bull and put it on some wood on an altar. "Call on your god to send fire," he said. The prophets of Baal called on their god for hours. They even cut themselves. But nothing happened.

Then Elijah cut up another young bull and put the pieces on the wood. He poured twelve barrels of water on it. Then Elijah prayed. Fire flashed from heaven and burned up the offering. It even burned up the stone altar.

The people of Israel fell to the ground and worshiped the Lord. Then Elijah commanded them to execute the prophets of Baal.

"Rain will come now!" Elijah told the king. Then he prayed. Before long a powerful rainstorm came. The famine would soon be over.

When King Ahab went home, he told wicked Queen Jezebel what had happened. Jezebel should have been afraid of the Lord. Instead, she sent a message to Elijah. "I will kill you by this time tomorrow," she warned.

Elijah should have known the Lord would take care of him. Instead he ran for his life into the wilderness. He sat under a bush and prayed to die. Then he went to sleep.

While Elijah was sleeping an angel touched him and told him to get up and eat. He looked around. There was some bread baking nearby, as well as some water. This happened twice.

Elijah traveled on until he reached Mount Sinai, where he lived for a while in a cave.

Elijah Listens to a Quiet Voice

One day the Lord asked Elijah why he was there.

"I am the only prophet left," Elijah said. "The Israelites have killed all the others."

The Lord told him to stand outside on the mountain. A great wind blew. But the Lord was not in the wind.

Then a mighty earthquake rumbled. But the Lord was not in the earthquake.

Then there was a fire. But the Lord was not in the fire.

At last there was a quiet whisper. The Lord was in the quiet whisper.

1 Kings 19:1-14

Go home," the Lord told Elijah. "Along the way anoint Hazael to be King of Syria. Then anoint Jehu to be the next King of Israel. Then anoint Elisha to take your place. And by the way, Elijah, there are actually 7,000 men in Israel who have never worshiped Baal!"

Elijah obeyed the Lord and went back. Along the way he found Elisha plowing a field with eleven teams of oxen ahead of him. Elijah went over and threw his cloak across Elisha's shoulders. Then he walked away.

Elijah Gives His Cloak to Elisha

848 B.C.

Elisha ran after him. "Please let me go back and say good-bye to my father and mother," he said. "Then I'll go with you."

Elijah said that would be all right.

Then Elisha killed his oxen. He used the wood from the plow to make a fire and roasted the meat of the oxen over the fire. Then he had a great feast for his plowmen. After that, Elisha left his work and went with Elijah to help him.

One day King Ahab asked Naboth if he could buy his vineyard, which was next door to the palace. Naboth said no, because the vineyard had been in his family for a long time. Now Ahab was in a grumpy mood.

"What's the matter?" Queen Jezebel asked. Ahab told her.

"Well, are you the king or aren't you?" she demanded. "I'll get that vineyard for you."

She arranged for two evil people to lie about Naboth. They

Ahab Steals Naboth's Vineyard

said he had cursed God and the king. He was dragged outside the city and stoned to death.

"The vineyard is yours," she said to Ahab.

So Ahab went to the vineyard to claim it, but Elijah was there with a message from the Lord. "You have killed Naboth and robbed him. Because of this, dogs will lick your blood outside the city just as they have licked Naboth's blood. Not one male in your family will be spared. You have led Israel into sin and made the Lord angry. Dogs will also tear apart the body of your wife Jezebel."

When Ahab heard these things, he tore his clothing. He humbled himself in rags before the Lord. So the Lord said to Elijah, "Because Ahab has humbled himself before Me, I will not bring those punishments during his lifetime. I will do them instead to his sons."

1 Kings 21

At last it was time for Elijah to go into heaven. Elijah and Elisha traveled together, first to Bethel, then to Jericho, then to the Jordan River.

While fifty young prophets watched from a distance, Elijah folded his cloak and hit the water with it. The river divided, and the two walked across on dry ground.

"What would you like from me before I leave?" Elijah asked Elisha.

"I want double the power of a prophet that you have," Elisha asked.

"That's hard," Elijah said. "But if you see me when I am taken, you will have it."

Suddenly a chariot of fire came down, pulled by horses of fire. It went between the two prophets. Elijah was carried into heaven in a whirlwind.

Elijah Goes Away in a Whirlwind

Elisha saw this and
cried out, "My
father! My father!
The chariots of Israel
and their horsemen!"

As Elijah, the chariot, and the
horses went out of sight, Elisha
tore his cloak.

Then he picked up Elijah's cloak,
went back to the Jordan River, and hit
the river with the cloak. The water divided,
and Elisha went across on dry ground.

2 Kings 2:1-18

A prophet died and left his widow without any money and with a large debt to pay. The man who had lent the money demanded that the widow pay it back. She didn't have the money, so this man was about to take her two sons as slaves.

"What do you have?" Elisha asked the widow.

"Nothing," she said. "All I have is a jar of oil."

"Go to your friends and neighbors and borrow all the pots and pans that you can," Elisha said. "Pour olive oil from your jar into these pots and pans."

Elisha Helps a Poor Widow

She began to pour the oil. Her sons brought her the pots and pans, and she kept on filling them from her jar of oil. As long as she poured, the oil kept on flowing. At last there were no more pots and pans to fill. Then the oil stopped flowing.

The widow told Elisha what had happened.

"Sell the oil and pay the debt," he said. "You will even have money left over for living expenses."

2 Kings 4:1-7

Elisha traveled about through the land. One day he visited Shunem, where a very important lady asked him to eat with her and her husband. They had such a good time that Elisha stopped there to eat whenever he was in town.

One day this lady had an idea. "Let's make a guest room for this prophet of God," she suggested to her husband. "We'll put a bed, table, chair, and lamp in the room, and it will always be ready for Elisha."

Elisha was thankful for his beautiful room. "Tell this woman I want to thank her," Elisha said to his servant Gehazi, "and ask her what we can do for her."

A Room for Elisha

"Nothing," was the woman's answer. "I'm happy with everything we have."

When she left, Elisha asked Gehazi what he thought. "What can we do for her?"

"She and her husband have no son," Gehazi answered. "The husband is too old."

Elisha told Gehazi to ask the woman back to see him. "Next year you will have a son," he said.

"Oh, don't lie to me," she answered. But it happened as Elisha had said. The next year the woman had a baby boy. She was so happy that God had worked a miracle in her life.

2 Kings 4:8-17

The miracle baby boy grew older. One day he went to the fields to see his father. Suddenly he had a bad headache. The father told a servant to carry him home, but by noon the boy had died.

His mother carried him to Elisha's bed, then sent word to her husband. "Send a servant home with a donkey," she begged. "I must go to see the prophet." She rode the donkey as fast as she could.

Near Mount Carmel Elisha saw her coming. "Run to meet her," Elisha told Gehazi. "Ask her what the problem is."

When the woman came to Elisha, she fell at his feet. "You promised me a son," she said. "I told you not to lie to me."

Elisha Raises a Boy from the Dead

Then Elisha knew that the boy had died. "Hurry, take my staff," he told Gehazi. "Put it on the boy's face." Gehazi went ahead and did as Elisha said, but nothing happened.

When Elisha arrived, he went into his room and stretched himself over the boy. He went downstairs, came back, and stretched himself over the child again. The boy sneezed seven times and opened his eyes.

Now Elisha called Gehazi. "Bring his mother here," he said. When she came in, Elisha said to her, "Here is your son."

The woman fell down before Elisha. Then she took her little boy and walked out with him.

2 Kings 4:18-37

*E*lisha had asked for twice
the miracle-working power of Elijah.
Already he had told how a child would be born to old parents, then
had raised that child from the dead. When a young prophet accidentally put
poisonous gourds in a stew, Elisha made it right again. Another time he helped
feed a hundred prophets with twenty loaves of barley bread. His next miracle was
one of healing.

Naaman was an important Syrian general who had leprosy. In one of his conquests,
Naaman had captured a little Israelite girl, who helped care for his wife. One day she
said to Naaman's wife, "If only my master would go to see Elisha, he could be
healed."

So the King of Syria sent his general Naaman to the King of Israel with
a letter saying, "I want you to heal Naaman."

Naaman Is Healed

"Does he think I'm God?" the king said, panicking. But Elisha heard about it and said to send Naaman to him.

Naaman came and stood at Elisha's door. Elisha sent a servant out to tell Naaman to wash seven times in the Jordan River, and he would be healed.

Naaman was insulted. "At least he could have come out to talk with me," he complained. "If I need to wash in a river, I'll go home and do it." But Naaman's officers begged him to do what Elisha said.

So Naaman went to the Jordan River and dipped himself in it seven times. At once he was completely healed.

2 Kings 5:1-14

During the times of Elijah and Elisha, most of the kings of Israel and Judah were evil.

While Joram, son of Ahab, was King of Israel, Elisha told another young prophet to find Jehu and anoint him as king. "You must destroy Ahab's whole family," the young prophet told Jehu.

Jehu jumped into a chariot and raced to find King Joram, then shot him with an arrow. Then he chased Ahaziah, the King of Judah, and shot him too. Next Jehu raced for the palace and saw Joram's mother, the wicked Queen Jezebel, sitting in a window. He called to some young men behind her, and they threw her to the ground. Then Jehu had Ahab's seventy sons executed, as well as the priests of Baal.

But after all that, Jehu didn't follow the Lord either. He worshiped golden calves.

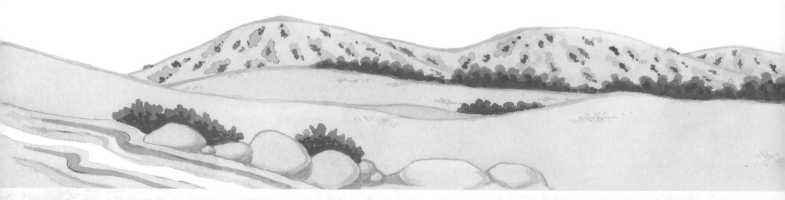

Joash the Boy King

Meanwhile, in Judah, the wicked mother of King Ahaziah heard that he was dead. She killed all his children, her own grandchildren, so she could rule. But Ahaziah's sister hid one grandson, little Joash, for six years. In the seventh year, Joash was revealed and made king. The wicked queen was executed.

The high priest led the people in dedication to the new king and to the Lord. They broke down the heathen altars and the temple of Baal. At last the city of Jerusalem was peaceful. The Lord was honored by the seven-year-old king and his people.

2 Kings 11; 2 Chronicles 22:10–23:21

*J*ehu ruled Israel for twenty-eight years. He destroyed much of the evil influence of foreign gods, but he didn't destroy the golden calves that people worshiped. Meanwhile in Judah, Joash was ruling. Both kings did many good things. But they left some evil things for their people.

During the years of evil kings, the great temple that Solomon had built in Jerusalem was neglected. Judah's young King Joash gave orders to Jehoiada, the high priest, to gather money and hire carpenters, masons, and quarrymen to repair the temple.

Also during Joash's rule, the King of Syria came against Judah. Joash took gold from the temple

Joash Repairs the Temple

800 B.C. Ship building begins in Greece

and paid the King of Syria to leave them alone. So the King of Syria went home.

Joash ruled Judah for forty years, then was killed by two of his trusted officers. His son Amaziah became king in his place. He was a good king, as Joash had been. But, like Joash, he failed to destroy the pagan shrines in the hills.

Joash's grandson and great-grandson were also good kings, but they were followed by a wicked king. When he died, Joash's descendant Hezekiah became king over Judah. He too was a good king and trusted the Lord completely.

2 Kings 12:1-16; 2 Chronicles 24–28

The Lord ordered the Prophet Jonah to go to Nineveh, the capital of Assyria. "Tell them I will destroy them because they are so wicked."

Assyria was big and powerful, a hated enemy of Israel, with cruel leaders. Jonah was afraid. So when the Lord had told him to go east, he went west, leaving on a ship for Tarshish.

A great storm came over the sea. The captain found Jonah asleep and ordered him to pray. Then the crew drew straws to see who had done something wrong. It was Jonah.

The Story of Jonah

793 B.C. Jonah begins to prophesy

"What have you done?" they asked. "I'm running away from God," he answered. "What should we do?" "Throw me into the sea," Jonah answered. So they did.

But the Lord had prepared a big fish to swallow Jonah. Inside the fish, he prayed and promised to obey the Lord. So the Lord had the fish spit Jonah out onshore. "Now go to Nineveh," the Lord commanded.

This time Jonah obeyed. "Forty days from now the Lord will destroy Nineveh," Jonah preached. Everyone, even the King of Assyria, repented.

So God decided not to destroy Nineveh. This made Jonah angry. As he sat under the hot sun, the Lord caused a plant to grow over him and give him shade. Then a worm destroyed the plant, and Jonah was angry again. The Lord told him, "You felt sorry for the plant. Shouldn't I feel sorry for a city of 120,000 people?"

The Book of Jonah

Now is the time to stop and look back at the sad story of Israel.

David had been a wonderful king, and the Lord blessed the nation because he was faithful. At first his son, King Solomon, pleased the Lord. But his many pagan wives turned his heart from the Lord to worship foreign gods. So the Lord caused the kingdom to divide.

Jeroboam ruled the ten tribes, called Israel. He was the first of nineteen kings who ruled Israel for about 200 years. But every one of them except Jehu was evil—and even Jehu let the people worship pagan gods. So the Lord was patient for 200 years, but His patience was coming to an end.

This is the story about the ten tribes of Israel and how they were carried away from their homeland. About seventy years before this story, Jonah had been a prophet. Hosea prophesied

Israel Is Taken into Captivity

743 B.C. Assyria invades Israel

about thirty years before this story. Isaiah began to prophesy just before this story.

During the reign of Hoshea, Assyria attacked Israel and made Israel pay heavy taxes. Then King Hoshea rebelled. He asked Egypt to help him fight Assyria. When the king of Assyria heard that, he put Hoshea in prison. Assyria conquered Israel and sent many Israelite people to Assyria. This happened because the Israelites had worshiped pagan gods and forgotten the one true God. The Lord sent prophets to warn them, but they would not change. So finally He permitted Assyria to take them into captivity. The Assyrians sent other captive people to occupy the land of Israel.

Many of these people tried to worship both their gods and the God of Israel. But the Lord is not pleased with that kind of worship, is He?

When the twelve tribes were divided into ten and two, the two tribes became the Kingdom of Judah. This kingdom lasted longer than the Kingdom of Israel, because Judah had several good kings who pleased the Lord. One of these was Hezekiah.

When Hezekiah died, his son Manasseh ruled Judah for fifty-five years, but he was an evil king. So was his son Amon, whose servants killed him after two years. Then Amon's son Josiah, who was only eight years old, became king.

The Book of the Law Is Found and Read

When Josiah was twenty-six, he gave orders for the temple to be repaired, just as Joash had done many, many years before. One day the high priest found a scroll. "It has God's laws written on it," he said. He showed it to the king's secretary, who then read it to King Josiah.

"We have not been following God's laws," Josiah said to the leaders of the temple. "What should we do?"

Then the Lord sent word by a prophetess: "Because Judah has turned against Me, I will destroy Judah and Jerusalem. But because you have followed Me, I will not do this until after you die."

Josiah called the leaders and people to the temple. There he read God's Word to them. He and the people promised to follow the Lord. They destroyed the evil places of worship. As long as Josiah was king, Judah honored the Lord and worshiped Him only.

2 Kings 22:1–23:27; 2 Chronicles 34:1–35:19

Assyria had been a great empire, but now it was getting weaker. Egypt went to war against Assyria, which had ruled over them. For some strange reason Josiah fought against Egypt. In the battle King Josiah was badly wounded. His troops brought him back to Jerusalem, where he died.

Josiah's son Jehoahaz was the new king. But he ruled only three months before the King of Egypt put him in prison, where he died. Egypt now demanded taxes and tribute from Judah.

The King of Egypt made Jehoahaz's brother, Jehoiakim, the new king. He was an evil king, and during his reign, King Nebuchadnezzar of Babylon attacked Jerusalem. He took Jehoiakim in chains to Babylon.

Then Jehoiakim's son, Jehoiachin, became king for three months.

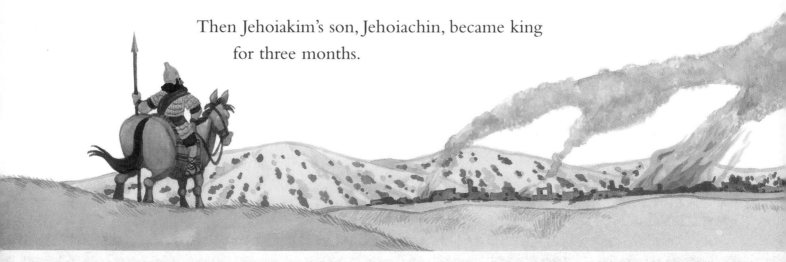

Judah Falls and Jerusalem Is Destroyed   586 B.C.

During that time, the armies of Babylon came back and put Jehoiachin into prison. They took all the temple treasure and 10,000 captives, including the princes and skilled people. Daniel and his friends were taken to Babylon about this time.

The next king of Judah was Zedekiah, who was only twenty-one years old. He too was an evil king. Nebuchadnezzar captured and killed him and his sons.

The Babylonians burned the temple and destroyed Jerusalem. It had been 135 years since Israel (the ten tribes) was defeated and carried into exile. Now Judah (the two tribes) was defeated and carried into exile. Only the very poor were left to farm the land.

2 Kings 23:29–25:21; 2 Chron. 36:11-23; Jeremiah 39; 52

Before Judah was taken to Babylon, Jeremiah was called to be a prophet. God's first message to Jeremiah came during the reign of King Josiah; others came during the reign of Josiah's son Jehoiakim.

One of God's messages came during the fourth year of Jehoiakim's reign. "Write My messages on a scroll," the Lord commanded. So Jeremiah dictated the Lord's messages to the scribe Baruch, who wrote them on a scroll.

King Jehoiakim Burns Jeremiah's Scroll

"Read these in the temple," Jeremiah commanded. When Baruch did so, a man named Micaiah went to tell some leaders what he had heard. They wanted to hear too. So Baruch read Jeremiah's scroll to them.

"You and Jeremiah had better hide," the leaders said. "We're going to tell the king about the scroll."

King Jehoiakim was sitting near an open fire as he listened to the words of the scroll. Not only did he show no sign of fear or repentance, but each time the reader finished a part of the scroll, the king cut that part off and threw it into the fire!

But the Lord spoke to Jeremiah again and told him to make another scroll. So again Jeremiah told Baruch what to write on the scroll. Then he sent word to King Jehoiakim that Babylon would destroy Judah. The king would be killed, along with his officials. Not one of Jehoiakim's descendants would be king for a long time.

Jeremiah 1; 36

Zedekiah, King of Judah, would not listen to the Lord's messages through Jeremiah.

One day as Jeremiah was walking through the city gate, a guard grabbed him. He accused Jeremiah of going to join the Babylonians. The city officials had Jeremiah beaten and put into prison.

Later King Zedekiah secretly sent for Jeremiah. "Is there a message from the Lord?" he asked.

"Yes," said Jeremiah. "The King of Babylon will defeat you." Then Jeremiah begged the king not to send him back to the prison where he had been, so Zedekiah put him

Ebed-Melech Rescues Jeremiah

into the palace prison instead. But some men were angry at the things Jeremiah had said. They told the king that Jeremiah must die.

So Zedekiah gave these men permission to do what they wanted. They took Jeremiah from the palace prison and let him down into an empty well with mud at the bottom.

A palace official named Ebed-Melech heard what had happened. He begged the king to let him rescue Jeremiah. The king agreed, so Ebed-Melech went with thirty men and pulled Jeremiah out of the well. Then Jeremiah stayed in the palace prison until Jerusalem was captured and destroyed.

*D*aniel and his three friends (whom the Babylonians called Shadrach, Meshach, and Abednego) were probably teenagers when Jerusalem was destroyed. They were among the thousands who were forced to go to Babylon during the three-month reign of Jehoiachin. At the orders of King Nebuchadnezzar, these young men from Judah's royal family were put into a three-year program to become leaders in Babylon.

They were given the best training and the best food. But Daniel asked his teacher to let the four of them eat vegetables and water instead of rich food and wine. "Let us try this for ten days," Daniel said.

Daniel Refuses to Eat the King's Food

"Then you can see how we look and decide what to do."

The man in charge agreed. At the end of the ten days, the four looked even healthier than the others in training. They were allowed to stay on a diet of vegetables and water.

The young men learned fast and became very wise. Daniel even had the ability to understand dreams and visions. At the end of the three-year training, Daniel and his three friends were brought to King Nebuchadnezzar. He gave them exams and was thrilled with what he heard. They were the best!

So he made Daniel and the other three his advisers. Their advice was ten times better than the advice of anyone else.

Daniel 1

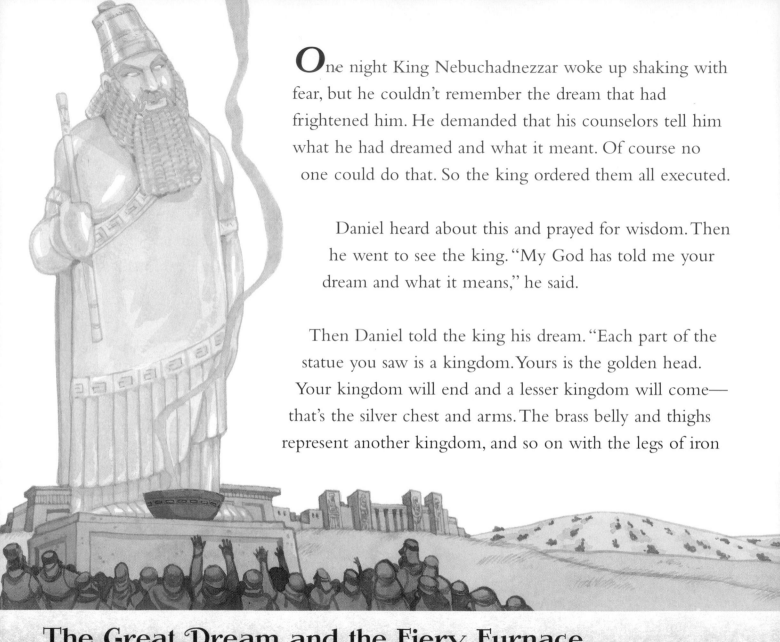

One night King Nebuchadnezzar woke up shaking with fear, but he couldn't remember the dream that had frightened him. He demanded that his counselors tell him what he had dreamed and what it meant. Of course no one could do that. So the king ordered them all executed.

Daniel heard about this and prayed for wisdom. Then he went to see the king. "My God has told me your dream and what it means," he said.

Then Daniel told the king his dream. "Each part of the statue you saw is a kingdom. Yours is the golden head. Your kingdom will end and a lesser kingdom will come—that's the silver chest and arms. The brass belly and thighs represent another kingdom, and so on with the legs of iron

The Great Dream and the Fiery Furnace

and feet of iron and clay. But in time there will be a kingdom that will never end."★

Some time later Nebuchadnezzar built a big statue and ordered everyone to bow down before it. "Anyone who does not will be thrown into a fiery furnace," he declared. Shadrach, Meshach, and Abednego refused to bow down.

The king was furious. "Bow down or I'll throw you into the flames!" he commanded. But they would not.

The king ordered men to make the furnace seven times hotter than usual. But when the three friends were thrown in, they didn't burn. The king could see a fourth person in the fire with them. Now the king knew that God had spared them. He promoted them to high places and commanded people to worship their God.

★The great kingdom that would never end, of course, referred to
Christ's kingdom.

*A*t the time of this story, Daniel had lived in Babylon for sixty-six years, through the reign of six different kings. The current ruler was Belshazzar, one of Nebuchadnezzar's descendants.

One night Belshazzar gave a big party. He invited 1,000 officers. To make the party more exciting, he brought out the gold and silver cups that had been taken from the temple in Jerusalem. The king and his guests drank wine from these cups, celebrating their pagan gods.

Suddenly a great hand appeared and began to write on the wall. King Belshazzar was terrified. "Bring someone to read this writing," the king ordered. "I will give that person great honor." But no one could read the writing.

Handwriting on the Wall

Then Daniel was brought in. "I'll give you great honor if you can read that," Belshazzar said.

"Keep your gifts," Daniel said. "I will read it anyway. You know about the Lord, but you have defied Him. You have praised pagan gods while drinking from temple cups. The words *mene mene tekel parsin* mean you have been weighed on God's scales and have failed His test. Your kingdom will be divided and given to Medes and Persians."

Belshazzar honored Daniel. But that same night he was killed. Darius captured the city. The great Babylonian Empire had come to an end.

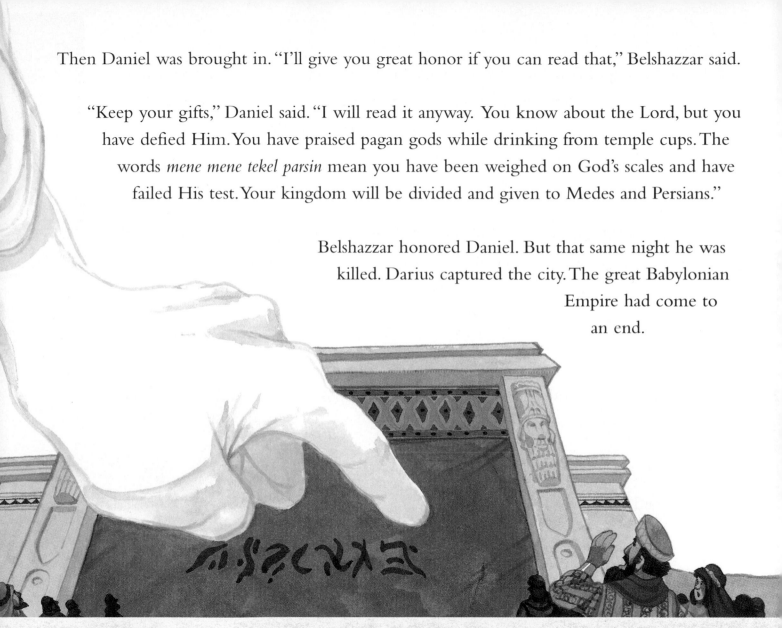

Daniel 5

*T*he next King of Babylon, Darius, divided the kingdom into 120 provinces and put a governor over each. These governors reported to three great rulers, one of whom was Daniel. The other two were jealous of Daniel, so they tried to find something wrong with him. They persuaded King Darius to make a new law that for thirty days, no one could ask a favor of any god or man except the king.

But Daniel would not stop praying to God. He prayed three times each day, with his windows open toward Jerusalem. The other rulers ran to tell the king what Daniel was doing. King Darius was angry with himself for making such a foolish law, but even he could not change it.

At last he had Daniel arrested and thrown into a den of lions. "May the God you worship save you," he said. That night the king could not eat or sleep.

Early the next morning the king ran to the lions' den and called, "O Daniel,

Daniel in the Lions' Den

was your God able to save you?"

Daniel answered, "My God sent an angel to shut the lions' mouths. I have done nothing wrong."

The king had Daniel taken out of the lions' den. There was not a scratch on him. Then he had the men who had accused Daniel thrown into the lions' den, along with their families. King Darius sent a message throughout his empire: "Fear the God of Daniel."

Daniel 6

*I*t seems as if the Israelites were nearly always at war, from the days when they fought different tribes to occupy the Promised Land to the conquering of Judah by the Babylonians. Eventually Cyrus of Persia defeated the Babylonians, and the Persians became the great world power.

Both the Assyrians and Babylonians had been cruel leaders. When they conquered a nation they deported its people and scattered them.

But Cyrus was kinder. He let about 43,000 people of Israel, mostly the people of Judah, return to the Promised Land. The people went to Jerusalem first and began to rebuild the

The People Return Home

temple. But their neighbors resisted and the work stopped for fifteen years, until Darius became the Persian ruler.

The Prophets Haggai and Zechariah encouraged Darius, and he even gave the Israelites money to complete the temple. Work on the rest of Jerusalem went on for about seventy years. Then Ezra, a priest, went to Jerusalem and made the people stop marrying pagan wives. He also started synagogue worship.

The story that comes next, Queen Esther's story, happened back in the land of captivity during the time of Ezra.★

★The story of Esther takes place between the events of Chapters 6 and 7 of the Book of Ezra.

The Book of Ezra

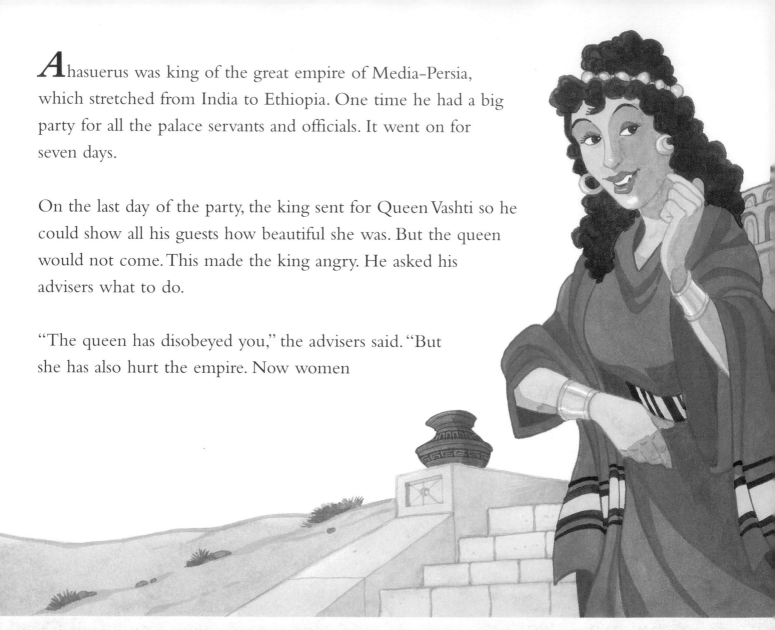

Ahasuerus was king of the great empire of Media-Persia, which stretched from India to Ethiopia. One time he had a big party for all the palace servants and officials. It went on for seven days.

On the last day of the party, the king sent for Queen Vashti so he could show all his guests how beautiful she was. But the queen would not come. This made the king angry. He asked his advisers what to do.

"The queen has disobeyed you," the advisers said. "But she has also hurt the empire. Now women

Esther Becomes Queen

everywhere will disobey their husbands. You must send Queen Vashti away from you forever and choose a new queen."

The king liked that plan, so he sent word throughout his empire telling people what would happen. The search for a new queen began.

Mordecai was a Jew who had been captured when Babylon destroyed Jerusalem. He was taking care of a young cousin whose parents were dead. She was called Esther.

Esther was brought to the king's beauty contest. She was so beautiful and charming that the king fell in love with her and made her his new queen.

Esther 1-2

Haman was King Ahasuerus' prime minister, the second most powerful person in the empire. Everyone bowed when he went by . . . except Esther's cousin Mordecai. This made Haman angry. He decided to destroy all of Mordecai's people, the Jews.

Haman went to the king and lied about the Jews, saying that they refused to obey the king's laws and must be destroyed. So the king gave Haman permission to do it.

Mordecai was naturally very distressed by Haman's plan, and he told

Queen Esther Saves Her People

Esther she should go to the king and beg for her people. But no one, not even the queen, could go to see the king without an invitation. If she went to see him, she would be executed unless the king held out his golden scepter.

Esther took the chance. As she stood before the king, he held out his golden scepter. "What do you want, Queen Esther?" he asked.

"I want you and Haman to come to a banquet today," she said. At the banquet, the king asked Esther what she really wanted. "Come to another banquet tomorrow," she said. "Then I will tell you."

At the banquet the next day the king asked Esther again, "What do you want?" "Save me and my people," she cried.

"From whom?" the king asked. "Haman!" she said. "He wants to kill us."

So the king had Haman hanged. He made Mordecai his new prime minister. Everyone loved him, for he did what was right for all the people.

Some visitors came from Jerusalem to the royal palace at Shushan in Persia. There Nehemiah, a Jew, was a cupbearer for King Artaxerxes, the stepson of Queen Esther.

The visitors told Nehemiah that Jerusalem was still in terrible shape. Nehemiah sat down and cried. Then he prayed.

One day when Nehemiah was serving the king, Artaxerxes asked, "Why are you so sad?"

Nehemiah had the courage to tell the king the truth. "Jerusalem is still in ruins," he said. "Please send me back there. Let me rebuild the city of my ancestors."

Nehemiah Returns Home

The king agreed. Then Nehemiah asked for letters to the governors to let him go through their lands. He also asked for wood from the forests. King Artaxerxes gave Nehemiah all that he wanted and sent troops along to protect him as well.

When Nehemiah reached Jerusalem, he found enemies. Some officials did not want anyone to rebuild Israel. One night Nehemiah went around Jerusalem with a few men to look at things. The next day he went to see the city leaders. He asked them to help him rebuild the walls of Jerusalem.

"Good!" they said. "Let's do it." So they all went to work.

Nehemiah 1–2

Nehemiah divided the work of rebuilding the walls among many different groups. But two men, Sanballat and Tobiah, were angry and made fun of the wall builders. They even threatened to lead an army against them.

Nehemiah prayed for the Lord's help and guarded the city day and night. From that time on, half of the workers built the walls while the other half guarded. Even the workers kept weapons near them. People who lived outside Jerusalem moved into the city to be safe.

Nehemiah had another problem to solve too. Some rich Jews were taking advantage of the poor Jews. The poor

Nehemiah Builds the Walls of Jerusalem

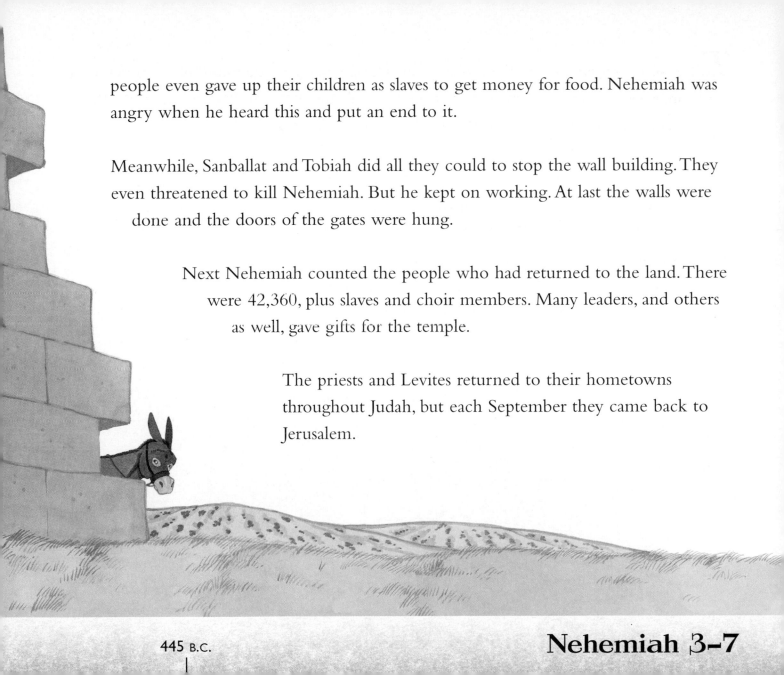

people even gave up their children as slaves to get money for food. Nehemiah was angry when he heard this and put an end to it.

Meanwhile, Sanballat and Tobiah did all they could to stop the wall building. They even threatened to kill Nehemiah. But he kept on working. At last the walls were done and the doors of the gates were hung.

Next Nehemiah counted the people who had returned to the land. There were 42,360, plus slaves and choir members. Many leaders, and others as well, gave gifts for the temple.

The priests and Levites returned to their hometowns throughout Judah, but each September they came back to Jerusalem.

Nehemiah 3–7

The walls of Jerusalem were complete now. The people were thankful. They gathered in front of the Water Gate and asked Ezra to read God's law to them. Ezra brought out the scroll, stood on a wooden stool, and read all morning. The people lifted their hands toward heaven, bowed, and worshiped the Lord. As Ezra read, God's helpers the Levites went among the people and explained what it meant. It was a day of great joy. At last the people had heard and understood God's words.

The next day the leaders, priests, and Levites met with Ezra. They studied the law more carefully. They read about the Feast of Tabernacles, when the people would live in tents. Then

Ezra Reads the Law

they sent messages throughout the land telling the people to go into the hills and gather branches to make booths like tents.

Before long there were little booths made of sticks everywhere. Some were on the rooftops of houses, others in courtyards, and others near the temple. During the seven days of the feast, the people lived in these little booths. Everyone celebrated with great joy. This had not been done since the time of Joshua, hundreds of years before.

On each of the seven days, Ezra read from God's law. Then on the eighth day there was a solemn service to end the feast.

Nehemiah 8

*B*etween the end of the Old Testament story and the beginning of the New Testament story is a period of about 400 years. What happened during these years?

The Old Testament closes with the Persian Empire ruling the world. The stories of Daniel in the lions' den, Ezra, Esther, and Nehemiah are all part of the time of the Persian Empire, which lasted until about 330 B.C.

Then a Greek ruler, Philip of Macedon, brought all the little Greek "city-states" together into one great nation. In 336 B.C. Philip died and his son Alexander took over. Alexander was a great military leader. In five short years he had conquered the entire known world. No wonder he was called Alexander the Great. Alexander brought Greek culture and language all over the world, which is why, eventually, the New Testament would be written in Greek.

But when Alexander was only thirty-two,

Between the Old and New Testaments

he died from malaria. His empire split into four parts, each ruled by a general. For a while after Alexander, Palestine was ruled by Syrians. Then the Ptolemies, Egyptian kings, ruled. Then a wicked Syrian ruler recaptured Palestine. Syrian rule was cruel.

One Syrian ruler, Antiochus Epiphanes, tried to wipe out the Jews and their religion. But a group of warlike Jews rebelled. One great Israelite leader, Judas Maccabeus, took Jerusalem from the Syrians. That began the Maccabean period of about 100 years, when the Jews ruled their own land.

Then, in 63 B.C., the Romans conquered Palestine. They ruled over Palestine at the time of the New Testament events. The Romans built great roads all over the world. Although the Romans didn't know it, these very roads would make it easier for the Gospel to be spread. The world was now ready for Jesus Christ to come.

When Herod was king of Judea, a Jewish priest named Zacharias lived in Israel with his wife, Elizabeth. She was a descendant of Aaron, Moses' brother. Both Zacharias and Elizabeth were godly people who obeyed God's laws. But they had no children and were now too old to have any.

One year Zacharias had the honor of burning incense in the inner sanctuary of the temple in Jerusalem. While he did this, a large crowd waited outside, praying. Suddenly an angel appeared to Zacharias.

"Don't be afraid," the angel said. "You and Elizabeth will have a son. You must name him John. He will be a great

An Angel Tells about John's Birth

man of God. He will prepare people for the coming of the Messiah, the Son of God."

"But Elizabeth and I are too old to have a child," Zacharias said.

The angel answered, "I am Gabriel! I stand in God's presence. He has sent me to tell you this. But since you didn't believe me, you will not be able to talk until the baby is born."

Zacharias stayed at the temple until his term for service was over, then he went home to the hill country. Soon after that Elizabeth knew she would have a baby. Of course she was thrilled.

"How kind the Lord is," she said.

Luke 1:5-25

Three months later, the Angel Gabriel visited a young lady named Mary, who lived in the village of Nazareth in Galilee. Mary was engaged to a man named Joseph, a descendant of King David.

"Blessings on you, favored lady," Gabriel said. "The Lord is with you." But Mary was confused. What could the angel mean?

"Don't be afraid, Mary," Gabriel continued. "The Lord will bless you in a most unusual way. You will have a baby boy and will name Him

An Angel Tells about Jesus' Birth

Jesus. He will be called the Son of God. The Lord will give him David's throne, and He will rule over Israel forever. His kingdom will never end."

"But I'm not married yet," Mary answered. "How can I have a baby?"

"The Holy Spirit will come to you," Gabriel answered. "God will be the child's true Father. Jesus will be the Son of God."

"I am the Lord's servant," Mary said. "I will do exactly what He wants."

Gabriel also told Mary that her cousin Elizabeth was expecting a child. A few days later, Mary went to visit her. Elizabeth's baby leaped inside her when she heard Mary's voice.

Luke 1:26-56

The news spread to the neighbors that Elizabeth had a baby boy. Everyone was so happy. Eight days later it was time for the boy to be circumcised and named. Zacharias still could not speak, but Elizabeth told everyone, "The baby's name must be John."

The neighbors were surprised by this, so they asked Zacharias about it. He motioned for a tablet to be brought, and wrote on it, "His name is John."

John the Baptist Is Born

At that very moment, Zacharias could talk again. He began to praise the Lord.

A great sense of awe swept through the neighborhood. The people realized that the Lord was doing something special. "What will this boy do when he grows up?" they wondered.

Zacharias was filled with the Holy Spirit, and he gave a special prophecy. "Praise the Lord," he said. "He is sending a Mighty Savior as He promised long ago."

Then Zacharias spoke to little John. "You, little child, will make people ready for the Messiah, God's Son. You will help people find salvation through forgiveness of sins."

As John grew up, he loved the Lord very much. He lived in the desert until he began his minsitry.

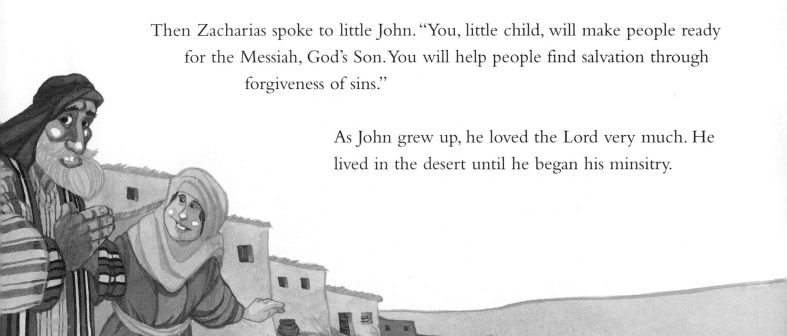

Luke 1:57-80

Mary was engaged to be married to Joseph. But now she was expecting a child. This troubled Joseph, for he was a good man. He thought Mary must have been unfaithful to him. There seemed to be no other explanation.

According to the rules of their society, Joseph could have chosen to have Mary stoned to death. But he loved her too much to do

An Angel Talks with Joseph

that, so he decided just to quietly break their engagement.

One night Joseph was lying awake thinking about this. Then he began to dream. An angel was standing beside him.

"Joseph, don't be afraid to get married to Mary," the angel said. "She has not been unfaithful to you. The baby's father is truly the Holy Spirit. Mary will have a Son, and you will name Him Jesus. He will be the Savior, the Messiah. He will save His people from their sins, just as the prophets said."

When Joseph woke up, he did what the angel had said. He and Mary were married. But he did not sleep with her until Jesus was born.

Matthew 1:18-25

At this time Rome ruled the land where Mary and Joseph lived. About the time that Mary's baby was due to be born, the Roman Emperor Caesar Augustus made a law. All people must go to the home of their ancestors to register. Augustus wanted a census, or counting, of the whole empire.

Joseph was a member of King David's royal line, so he had to go to Bethlehem in Judea to be counted. (Bethlehem was,

Jesus Is Born

6-5 B.C.

of course, the childhood home of King David. He had cared for his father's sheep on the hillsides outside the village.)

Joseph took Mary with him, even though she was almost ready to have her baby. When they reached Bethlehem, there was no more room in the village inn. The only room available was in the stables, where animals were kept. So Mary and Joseph stayed there.

That night Mary had her Baby Boy. She wrapped Him in strips of cloth and put Him down to sleep in a manger.

World population estimated at 250 million

Luke 2:1-7

*T*he night that Jesus was born some shepherds were guarding their sheep on the hillsides just outside of Bethlehem. Suddenly an angel appeared to them. The hills were lit up with the glory of the Lord. Naturally the shepherds were scared, but the angel comforted them.

"Don't be afraid," the angel said. "I have wonderful news—the most joyful news ever told. The Messiah has been born in Bethlehem. You may go to see Him. He is lying in a manger, wrapped in strips of cloth."

Angels Appear to Some Shepherds

Then the angel was joined by a great choir of angels. It seemed as if the armies of heaven were all there, praising the Lord. "Glory to God in the highest heaven," they sang. "Peace has come to earth for all who please Him." Then the angel choir disappeared into heaven.

The shepherds were alone again. "Let's go!" they shouted. "Let's go to see this great thing the Lord has shared with us."

So the shepherds found Mary and Joseph. They saw the Baby lying in a manger. Then they went out to tell everyone what they had seen. They praised the Lord that they had seen this Child.

Mary had much to think about. She quietly wondered about all these things for a long, long time.

Luke 2:8-20

*W*hen Baby Jesus was eight days old, Mary and Joseph brought Him to the temple to be circumcised and named. Of course they named Him Jesus, as that was what the Angel Gabriel had said to do.

As they came into the temple, they met an old man named Simeon. He was a godly man, filled with the Holy Spirit, who had been waiting for years for the Messiah to come. The Holy Spirit had told him that he would not die before he saw the Messiah.

Simeon was waiting as Mary and Joseph came in, because the Holy Spirit had told him to be there. When he saw Baby Jesus, he knew that He was the Messiah. He took the child into his arms and began praising God. "Lord, now I can die happy,"

Simeon and Anna See Jesus

he said. "I have seen Your promised Messiah. He is the Savior, the Light of the World, the glory of Your people Israel."

Mary and Joseph stood there, amazed at what they heard. Then Simeon blessed them. He said to Mary, "You will also be deeply hurt because of this Child. Many will reject Him. But He will be great joy to many others."

Anna, a prophetess who was eighty-four, was also there in the temple. She stayed at the temple all the time, praying and often fasting. She came along as Simeon was talking, and she too began thanking the Lord. She told everyone she could that the Messiah had come.

Luke 2:21-38

Jesus was born in Bethlehem when Herod was king. About that time some wise men from eastern lands came to Jerusalem. "Where is the new King of the Jews?" they asked. "We saw His star when we were far away and have come to worship Him."

Herod was not pleased to hear that a new king had been born. He intended to be king for a long time to come. So he called some religious leaders together. "Did the prophets say where a new king would be born?" he asked.

Wise Men Visit Jesus

"Yes," they answered. "In Bethlehem, in Judea. Micah wrote about it. He said a ruler would come from that village and rule Israel."

So Herod sent for the wise men and told them what he had learned. Then he told them to go to Bethlehem and find the child, and then let him know. "Then I can worship Him too," Herod said. But he really wanted to kill Baby Jesus, not worship Him.

The wise men set out for Bethlehem. The star appeared again and led them right to the house where they found Mary and Baby Jesus. They bowed down and worshiped Him. Then they gave Him gifts of gold, frankincense, and myrrh.

But they went home another way, not through Jerusalem, for God had warned them in a dream not to go back to Herod.

Matthew 2:1-12

*W*hen the wise men had gone home, an angel of the Lord spoke to Joseph again. "King Herod will try to kill Jesus. You and Mary must take Him to Egypt. Stay there until I tell you to come home."

So they left that very night and lived in Egypt, just as the Prophet Hosea had said would happen.

Herod was angry when he realized that the wise men weren't coming back. He sent soldiers to Bethlehem to kill every baby boy two years old or younger (because the wise men had said the star appeared to them two years earlier). The Prophet Jeremiah had said this would happen.

Mary and Joseph Take Jesus to Egypt

Later, when Herod died, an angel of the Lord spoke to Joseph. "Take Mary and Jesus back to Israel," he said. "The people who wanted to kill Him are dead."

Joseph brought Mary and Jesus back to Israel. But along the way he was afraid. He had heard that Herod's son Archaelaus was the new king.

In another dream Joseph was warned not to go to Judea, but to go home to Galilee instead. So they settled down in the little village of Nazareth in Galilee. Some prophets had predicted that Jesus would be called a Nazarene.

Matthew 2:13-23

Jesus' real father was the Lord Himself. But Joseph cared for Jesus as if he were His father.

The Boy Jesus at Nazareth

Like every good Jewish father, Joseph taught Jesus a trade. Since he was a carpenter, he taught Jesus how to do carpentry work.

Joseph and Mary were godly people, and they also taught Jesus the Law, God's Word.

Jesus grew to be a strong young man. He was wiser than anyone else His age, but that's because He was God's Son. He knew things that no one else on earth knew.

God poured out His blessings on His Son. Someday Jesus would do wonderful things for God. But for now, He was a boy. It was His job to grow and learn.

Luke 2:39-40

*E*ach year faithful Israelite people went to Jerusalem for the Passover feast.

The year that Jesus was twelve, he went with Mary and Joseph. In those days people traveled in caravans, so children were often with relatives.

After the feast Mary and Joseph headed home. They must have thought Jesus was with friends or family, because a whole day went by before they missed Him.

Mary and Joseph went back to Jerusalem and looked for Jesus for three days. At last they found Him in the temple, sitting with the teachers of the Law and talking about thoughtful questions with them. Everyone was surprised by His answers.

When Mary and Joseph saw this they weren't sure what to think. "Why have You done

Jesus Teaches the Teachers

this to us?" Mary asked Jesus. "We have been frantically looking for You everywhere."

"But you didn't need to look in other places," Jesus answered. "You should have known that I would be here in the temple, my Father's house."

Mary and Joseph did not understand what Jesus meant. They should have remembered that God was His Father, and that Jesus had come to earth to do God's work.

Luke 2:41-52

In the Book of Isaiah, God promised to send His Son, the Messiah. He promised also that a special messenger would come first to prepare the world. God chose John, the son of Zacharias and Elizabeth, to be this messenger.

John was a rugged man who lived out in the desert. His clothing was made of camel's hair, and he had a leather belt around his waist. He ate locusts and wild honey.

John went along the Jordan River preaching that people should be baptized to show that they had turned from their sins. Many came to hear him. Some religious leaders also came.

John the Baptist Preaches

"Don't come here just to be baptized," John warned. "Turn from sin. Turn to God. Go out and prove you have changed by the way you live. Then I will baptize you."

Some people asked John if he was the Messiah, God's Son. "No, I am not," John answered.

"Are you Elijah?" they asked. "No," said John.

"Well, who are you?" they asked. "I am merely a messenger, sent to tell you that the Messiah is coming soon," John answered. "He is here right now among you. He is much greater than I am. I am not even worthy to be His slave or carry His shoes. I baptize you with water. He will baptize you with the Holy Spirit and fire."

Matthew 3:1-12; Mark 1:1-8; Luke 3:1-18; John 1:19-34

*J*esus came from Nazareth to the place where John was preaching near the Jordan River. When John saw Him coming, he shouted, "Look, there is the Lamb of God who takes away the sin of the world! I said that Someone was coming who lived long before me. I am pointing Him out to you and to the nation of Israel."

Jesus came to John to be baptized. At first John didn't want to baptize Jesus. "You should be baptizing me," he said.

But Jesus told John, "Please baptize Me. I must do all that is right to do." So John baptized Him.

Jesus Is Baptized

When Jesus came up out of the water, the heavens opened to Him. The Spirit of God came down on Jesus in the form of a dove.

God spoke from heaven with a mighty voice. "This is My Son. I love Him. I am very pleased with Him."

John said, "God told me that the Holy Spirit would rest on His Son like a dove. Now I know for sure that Jesus is God's Son. He will baptize you with the Holy Spirit."

Matthew 3:13-17; Mark 1:9-11; Luke 3:21-22

After Jesus was baptized, the Holy Spirit led Him out into the desert where Satan would tempt Him. Jesus ate nothing for forty days, so He was naturally very hungry.

The round stones nearby looked like loaves of bread. "Prove that You really are God's Son," Satan said. "Turn these stones into bread." It was Satan's trick to get Jesus to obey him.

"No," Jesus said. "The Scriptures say that other things are more important than bread. Bread will not feed our souls. We must obey God's Word."

Jesus Is Tempted

So Satan took Jesus to the highest place on the temple wall, called the pinnacle. "Prove that You are God's Son!" he said. "Jump off. The Scriptures say that God will send His angels to protect You. They will catch You and keep You from crashing into the rocks below."

Then Jesus quoted the Scriptures again. "God's Word says that you must not tempt God!"

Satan tried once more. He took Jesus into a high mountain. He showed Jesus the kingdoms of the world and all their glory. "I'll give all of this to You," Satan said. "All You must do is bow down and worship me."

"Go away, Satan!" Jesus answered. "The Scriptures say that we must worship and obey God only—not anything or anyone else."

Satan had lost. He went away, and angels came to take care of Jesus.

Matthew 4:1-11; Mark 1:12-13; Luke 4:1-13

One day John the Baptist was standing with Andrew and another of his followers when Jesus appeared. "Look," John said. "There is the Lamb of God." So John's followers left him and followed Jesus. "We want to see where You live," they said.

"Come with Me," said Jesus. They talked with Him all afternoon. Then Andrew left to find his brother Simon and bring him to Jesus. "We have found the Messiah," Andrew said.

"You are Simon," Jesus said. "From now on you will be called Peter. That means rock."

The next day Jesus headed back to Galilee. "Come with Me," He said to Philip, another follower. Philip first went to find Nathanael. "We have found the Messiah," he said, "the one Moses told us about. He is Jesus, son of Joseph,

Jesus Calls His First Disciples

A.D. 26-27 Jesus begins His ministry

from Nazareth." But Nathanael knew that Nazareth was just an ordinary little village. "Can anything good come from Nazareth?" he asked. "Come and see for yourself," Philip said.

When they came to Jesus, He said, "Here's an honest man, a true son of Israel."

"How do you know what I am like?" Nathanael asked. Jesus replied, "I saw you sitting under the fig tree before Philip found you." Now Nathanael was sure. "You really are God's Son."

"You believe in Me because I said that?" Jesus asked. "You will see much greater miracles. You will even see heaven open, and the angels of God going from heaven to earth on Me, the Messiah."

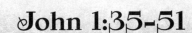
John 1:35-51

There was a big wedding in Cana of Galilee. Jesus and His mother, Mary, were among the wedding guests. Jesus' disciples were guests too.

During the feast the wine ran out. Mary came to Jesus and told Him the problem.

"But it's not quite time for Me to do miracles," He said.

Mary told the servants, "Do whatever He tells you."

Jesus Turns Water into Wine

So Jesus told the servants to fill the six big water pots nearby with water. Each one held about twenty to thirty gallons. "Take some to the master of the wedding," He said.

The master of the wedding tasted it. The water had become wine.

"This is wonderful," he told the bridegroom. "Usually a person starts with the best wine. But you have kept your best until the last."

So that was Jesus' first miracle. He proved His glory by doing it. The miracle helped His followers believe in Him.

John 2:1-11

On the feast of Passover the Israelites remembered the night that their ancestors were freed from slavery in Egypt.

Jesus went to Jerusalem for this feast. In the temple He saw merchants selling cattle, sheep, and doves for sacrifices. He saw moneychangers cheating the people who came to offer sacrifices.

Jesus was angry. He made a whip from ropes and drove the merchants out of the temple. He knocked over the moneychangers' tables.

Jesus Chases Bad Men from the Temple

"Get out of here!" He shouted. "Don't make My Father's house a marketplace."

When Jesus' followers saw this, they remembered a prophecy from the Psalms: "Your great love for God's house will eat you up."★

The religious leaders rushed up. "Who gave You the right to do this?" they demanded. "If You think God did, show us a miracle."

Jesus answered, "This is My miracle. Destroy this temple, and in three days I will rebuild it."

"It took forty-six years to build this temple," they scoffed. "How can you rebuild it in three days?" But Jesus was not talking about a building; He was talking about the temple of His body. Later, when Jesus was crucified and rose from the dead, the disciples remembered what He had said.   ★Psalm 69:9

John 2:13-25

Most of the religious leaders were against Jesus. They were jealous of His popularity. But one night Nicodemus, a leader of the group called the Pharisees, came to see Jesus. "We know that God has sent You to be our Teacher," he said. "Your miracles show us that."

"You must be born again," Jesus told him. "That is the only way you can get into heaven."

Nicodemus was puzzled. "How can I go back inside my mother and be born a second time?"

"People have babies," Jesus told him. "This birth brings us into our physical world. But to enter the spiritual world you must be born a different way. The Holy Spirit gives you this new birth. Don't be surprised when I tell you this. Listen to the wind! You hear it, but you can't tell where it came from or where it is going. That's the way it is when people are born again. It is spiritual birth through the Spirit of God."

Jesus Talks with Nicodemus

But Nicodemus still didn't understand.

"You are a great religious teacher," Jesus said.
"Why can't you believe what I am saying?
Just as Moses lifted a bronze snake
on a pole to save the people who
looked on it, so I will be lifted
up on a pole. I will die there
so people who believe in
Me will live forever. God
loved the world so much
that He sent Me, His only
Son. Whoever believes in
Me will not die spiritually,
but will live forever in
heaven."

John 3:1-21

One day Jesus stopped at a well in Samaria. A woman came to get water, and Jesus asked her for a drink. She was surprised that a Jewish man spoke to her. Jews hated Samaritans.

"If you knew who I am and what great gift God has for you," Jesus said, "you would ask Me for living water."

"Where would You get water?" she asked. "You don't have a bucket, and the well is deep. Anyway, how can You give me better water than this well?"

Jesus Talks with a Woman at a Well

"If you drink water from this well, you will get thirsty again," Jesus said. "If you drink the living water I give, you will never get thirsty again." Then the woman asked for some of the living water. "Bring your husband here," Jesus said.

"I'm not married," she answered. "That's true," said Jesus. "You have had five husbands, and the man you are living with now is not your husband."

"You must be a prophet," she said. "So where is it right to worship—Jerusalem, where you Jews worship, or Mount Gerizim, where we Samaritans worship?" Jesus answered, "It is not where we worship that counts, it is how we worship. You must worship the true God."

"The Messiah is coming," the woman said. "He will explain everything." "I am the Messiah," Jesus told her.

The woman ran back to the village and returned with a crowd. "He told me everything," she said. "Could He be the Messiah?" Then many Samaritans believed that Jesus was the Messiah.

John 4:4-42

When Jesus came back to Galilee, He was famous. People praised Him. They liked His sermons in the synagogues.

Once He preached at the synagogue in Nazareth, His childhood home. During the service, someone handed Him the Book of Isaiah to read. Jesus read the part that said, "He has chosen Me to preach Good News." Then he closed the scroll and gave it to the man who took care of it.

"These Scriptures came true today," He said. The people were surprised that Jesus spoke so well. "Isn't this Joseph's son?" they asked.

Jesus Preaches at the Nazareth Synagogue

"You may ask why I have not done miracles here in My hometown," Jesus said. "No prophet is honored in his hometown."

Then He preached about Jewish people who had done special things for foreigners. He talked about Elijah, who helped the widow in Sidon. He told of Elisha, who healed Naaman, the Syrian.

Now the people turned against Jesus. They did not want to hear that God had favored foreigners more than Jewish people.

Soon a mob came together. They pushed Jesus toward the edge of the cliff where Nazareth was built. But Jesus walked through the crowd and left them.

Luke 4:16-30

One day Jesus preached along the shore of the Sea of Galilee. Crowds pushed closer to hear Him.

Then Jesus saw fishermen washing their nets. They had two empty boats. Jesus got into one boat and asked the owner, Simon Peter, to go away from shore a little. There Jesus preached to the crowds on shore.

When Jesus finished preaching, He talked to Peter. "Let's go fishing where it is deeper," He said. "Let your nets down."

"We worked all night and caught nothing," Peter protested. "But if You want us to, we will do it."

Catching Fish with Jesus

Peter and his friends let the nets down. Soon the nets were filled with fish; in fact, they were so full that they began to tear.

Peter called for his friends in the other boat to help. Before long, both boats were full of fish.

Peter and his friends were amazed at what they had seen.

Peter fell on his knees before Jesus. "You should go away from me," he said. "I am a sinner and should not be near You."

Luke 5:1–9

Another day Jesus was walking along the shore of the Sea of Galilee. He saw Simon Peter and his brother Andrew fishing with their nets. They had a fishing business with two other brothers, James and John, sons of Zebedee.

"Come and follow Me," Jesus called to Simon Peter and Andrew. "I will help you fish for people."

So Simon Peter and Andrew left their nets behind and followed Jesus.

Jesus walked a little farther along the shore. He saw James and John sitting in a boat with

Jesus Calls Four Followers

their father Zebedee, fixing their nets. Jesus
called to them to follow Him.

So they left Zebedee and the hired helpers
and followed Jesus.

Now Jesus had His first four disciples.
They would follow Him
everywhere.

Matthew 4:18-22; Mark 1:16-20

*F*or a while Jesus was living in Capernaum. One day the house where He was staying was so crowded with people that there was not room for even one more.

Jesus was preaching in this crowded house when four more men came carrying a paralyzed friend. They tried to push through the crowd to get to Jesus, but they couldn't do it. So they dug a hole through the soft roof and let down the cot with the man on it, right into the room in front of Jesus! Jesus spoke to the paralyzed man. "Your sins are forgiven," He said.

This made some of the religious leaders angry. "This is blasphemy!" they said to each other. "Only God can forgive sins. Does Jesus think He is God?"

Jesus knew what these men were thinking. "Why should this trouble you?" He asked. "I am the Messiah, so I have power on earth to forgive sins. But why talk about it. I will prove what I say by healing this man."

Letting a Man Down through a Roof

Jesus spoke to the paralyzed man again. "Pick up your cot and go home. You are healed."

The man jumped up, picked up his cot, and walked home.

The people who saw this were amazed. They were also afraid. "We have never seen anything like this," they said.

Matthew 9:1-8; Mark 2:1-12; Luke 5:17-26

The people of Israel hated tax collectors because they gathered taxes for the Romans.

Matthew was one of these Jewish tax collectors. He had no friends among his fellow Jews.

One day Jesus came along the road where Matthew was working in his little tax collection booth.

"Come and follow Me," Jesus said to him. "Be My disciple."

Matthew didn't wait. He jumped up, left his

Jesus Calls Matthew

tax collection business, and followed Jesus.

That evening, Jesus and His disciples had dinner at Matthew's house. The guests included other tax collectors and sinful people.

The religious leaders were angry when they saw this. They complained to Jesus' disciples. "How can He do such a thing? How can He eat with such sinful people?" they asked.

Jesus heard what they said. "People who are well do not need a doctor," He said. "Sick people do. Now learn what God says in His Word. He does not want your sacrifices and gifts—He wants your heart to be merciful. I have not come to earth for those who think they have no sin. I have come to help sinners find their way to God."

Matthew 9:9-13; Mark 2:13-17; Luke 5:27-32

One day Jesus went up into the mountains. He stayed there all night, praying.

In the morning He called His followers together. Then He chose twelve of them to be His closest disciples. (Later they were called apostles.) They would go out preaching, healing, and making demons go away from people.

Here are the names of the twelve: Simon, who was also called Peter; his brother Andrew; James and John, the sons of Zebedee (Jesus sometimes

Jesus Chooses Twelve Disciples

called them "The Sons of Thunder"); Philip; Bartholomew; Matthew; Thomas; James the son of Alphaeus; Thaddaeus; and another Simon.

The other Simon was a member of a group called Zealots. This was a political party that encouraged rebellion against Rome.

There was also a man named Judas Iscariot. He was the one who would later betray Jesus.

Mark 3:13-19; Luke 6:12-16

One day a Roman army captain sent some Jewish leaders to see Jesus. His servant boy was sick; in fact, he was dying.

The captain asked Jesus to come and heal the boy.

"This is a good man," the Jewish leaders told Jesus. "He has even built a synagogue for us."

Jesus Heals a Centurion's Servant

Jesus started toward the man's home, but the captain sent another message to Jesus. "Please don't come to my home," the captain said. "I am not worthy to have You here. I am not even worthy to meet You. I have authority over people, so I know how great Your authority is. If You just say, 'Be healed,' the boy will be healed."

"I have never met a person with such great faith," Jesus said. "Even the Jewish people don't have that much faith."

The captain's friends went back to his house and found the boy completely healed.

Matthew 8:5-13; Luke 7:1-10

As Jesus went on with His disciples to the little village of Nain, crowds of people swarmed around Him.

As they came near the village gate, a funeral procession was coming out. A widow had lost her only son. Many of her friends and neighbors were weeping with her.

Jesus Raises a Widow's Son

Jesus felt sorry for her. "Please don't cry," He said. Then He went to the coffin, touched it, and spoke. "Young man, get up!"

The young man sat up and began to talk with the people around him. Then Jesus gave him back to his mother.

The crowd was stunned and afraid. They praised the Lord. "We have seen God work here today," they said.

News of this miracle raced like wildfire across Judea and even beyond to other regions.

Luke 7:11-17

Wherever Jesus went, crowds followed. Some people hoped to be healed. Some wanted to listen to Him teach.

One day Jesus went down to the shore of the Sea of Galilee. As usual, the crowds quickly gathered. Jesus got into a fishing boat and went a few feet from shore, where He taught the people from the boat.

Jesus did much of His teaching through stories. On this day He told a wonderful story about a farmer who planted seeds.

Jesus Teaches Parables from a Boat

Sowing these seeds was like sharing the Bible. The seeds fell on different kinds of soil, just as God's Word goes to different kinds of hearts.

Some soil is hard; some hearts are hard. Some soil is choked with weeds and thorns, so the seeds cannot grow; some hearts are cluttered with other things, so God's Word cannot grow. But some soil is good, and seeds will grow in it.

In the same way, some hearts listen. God's Word can take root and grow in them.

Matthew 13:1-23; Mark 4:1-20; Luke 8:4-15

Jesus finished teaching from the boat by evening. "Let's go to the other side of the lake," He said to His disciples. So they rowed away and left the crowd on shore. Some people got into boats and tried to follow.

But a great storm came suddenly on the Sea of Galilee. Waves crashed over the sides of the boat and it began to fill with water. It was about to sink.

Jesus Stills a Storm

The disciples woke Jesus, who was sleeping in the back of the boat. "Teacher, we are about to drown! Don't You care?" they shouted.

Jesus spoke to the wind and sea. "Be quiet," He said. The wind died down to a hush.

"Why were you so afraid?" Jesus asked the disciples. "Don't you trust Me?"

The disciples were afraid of what they had seen Jesus do. They whispered to one another. "Who is He? Even the wind and sea obey Him!"

Matthew 8:23-27; Mark 4:35-41; Luke 8:22-25

When Jesus reached the other side of the Sea of Galilee, a man rushed out and fell down before Him. This man was strong. When people tried to put him in chains, he would break them. Day and night he wandered around the hills or the tombs of the cemetery. Sometimes he screamed and cut himself with stones.

When Jesus saw this wild man, He commanded the demon in him to come out. The demon screamed, "What will You do with me, Jesus, Son of God? Don't torment me."

"What is your name?" Jesus asked. "Legion," the demon said. "There are really many of us."

Then the demons begged Jesus not to send them far away, but to let them go into some pigs nearby. So Jesus gave them permission to go into the pigs. When they did, the pigs rushed down the hill and drowned in the Sea of Galilee.

Jesus Heals a Man with a Demon

The men guarding the pigs ran into the nearby towns and told what had happened. Before long a great crowd gathered. There was the wild man, sitting peacefully by Jesus. The people were terrified. They begged Jesus to leave.

The man who had been healed wanted to go along, but Jesus told him to go home. "Tell people what great things the Lord has done for you," Jesus said. So that is what he did. He went all through that region, telling people about the Lord.

Matthew 8:28-34; Mark 5:1-20; Luke 8:26-39

When Jesus came back across the lake, a synagogue leader named Jairus bowed before Him. "My daughter is dying," he said. "But if You just touch her, she will live!"

Jairus and Jesus went toward his home. On the way a woman came behind Jesus and touched His robe. She had been bleeding inside for twelve years and had paid many doctors to try to heal her. *I must touch Jesus' clothes,* she thought. *If I do, I will be healed.* That is just what happened. As soon as she touched His robe, she was well.

Jesus knew that someone had been healed. He could feel the power go from Him.

"Who touched My clothes?" He asked.

Jesus Heals Jairus' Daughter

His disciples were surprised. "People are crowding all around You," they said. "How can You ask who touched Your clothes?"

But Jesus looked around for the person who had done it. Then the woman was afraid. She fell down before Jesus and told Him what had happened. "You are well because you believed," Jesus said to her.

By the time Jairus and Jesus reached his home, mourners had come to wail and make loud noises of sorrow.

"Get them out of here," Jesus said. "The girl is sleeping." But the people laughed and made fun of Him.

Jesus went where Jairus's twelve-year-old daughter was lying. He took the girl's hand. "Get up!" He said. And she jumped up and walked around the room.

Mark 5:21-43; Luke 8:40-56

Jesus went through many cities and villages, teaching about the kingdom of God. There were so many people with great needs, and they didn't know where to go for help. "We need more workers," Jesus said.

He gave His twelve disciples the power to heal and order demons out of people, then He sent them out to do His work.

"Go to the people of Israel," He said. "Tell them God's kingdom is near. Heal sick people, raise dead people, heal lepers, order demons from people.

Jesus Sends His Disciples Two by Two

"Don't take money with you. Let those you help feed you. Stay with godly people and bless their homes. Stay away from places that don't want you.

"You will be arrested and beaten. You will be tried by governors and kings. Tell them about Me. God will give you the right words to say.

"Don't be afraid of those who can kill your body. Fear God, for He can kill body and soul.

"Those who are faithful to the end will be saved. If you try to keep your life, you will lose it. If you give up your life for Me, you will keep it."

So Jesus sent the twelve out to teach and preach.

Matthew 9:35–11:1; Mark 6:7-13; Luke 9:1-6

*W*herever Jesus went, great crowds followed Him. Even when He tried to be alone, the crowds were always there.

One day He was healing some sick people and teaching the crowd about the kingdom of God. By late afternoon, the disciples were concerned. "It is getting late and we have no food for all these people," they said.

Jesus asked Philip, "Isn't there somewhere we can buy bread?" Jesus was testing him.

"There is nothing to eat out in this deserted place—and besides,

Jesus Feeds 5,000

it would cost a lot of money to feed all these people," Philip answered.

Andrew said to Jesus, "A little boy has five barley loaves and a couple of fish. But what can we do with that?"

"Tell the people to sit down for dinner," Jesus said. Then He took the little boy's lunch and thanked God for the food. He broke the bread and fish into pieces and gave them to the disciples to give to the people. Everyone had plenty to eat that evening. It was like a feast.

"Pick up the leftovers," Jesus said. When they did, the leftovers filled twelve baskets. Five thousand men, and many women and children, had dinner with Jesus that day!

The people were amazed. "He's the Messiah we have waited to see," they said. They tried to force Jesus to be their king, but He slipped away and went higher into the mountain to be alone.

Matt. 14:13-21; Mark 6:30-44; Luke 9:10-17; John 6:1-15

*B*efore Jesus went into the hills to pray, He told His disciples to get into the boat and go across the lake without Him. He would come later.

By this time it was night. Out on the Sea of Galilee, the disciples were having trouble. A storm had come up, and the wind was blowing hard and the waves were very high.

The disciples struggled with their boat in the stormy waves until about 4 o'clock in the morning. Suddenly they saw Jesus walking toward them on the water. They screamed in terror, because they thought He was a ghost!

"Don't be afraid," He called out.

Jesus Walks on Water

"Is it really You?" Peter called back. "Let me walk to You on the water."

When Jesus said it was all right, Peter climbed out of the boat and began walking toward Him. But when he looked around at the stormy waves, he got scared and began to sink. "Save me!" he cried.

Jesus took Peter by the hand and lifted him up. "You have so little faith," He said. "Why did you begin to doubt?"

As soon as Jesus climbed into the boat, the wind became quiet. The disciples were awestruck at what they had seen.

"You truly are the Son of God," they said.

Matthew 14:22-33; Mark 6:45-52; John 6:16-21

Jesus and His disciples were entering Bethsaida. Some people led a blind man to Him and begged Jesus to heal him.

Jesus led the man outside the village. There Jesus spat on the man's eyes, then He put His hands on them. "Can you see now?" Jesus asked.

"Yes, I can see people. But they are not clear. They look like trees," the man said.

Jesus Heals a Blind Man at Bethsaida

Jesus put His hands on the man's eyes again. Soon the man could see clearly. How wonderful it was to see after being blind.

Jesus told him to go home to his family without going back to Bethsaida.

Mark 8:22-26

One day Jesus took Peter, James, and John to the top of a high, lonely mountain. Jesus began to pray, and His three friends grew sleepy. But suddenly they were wide-awake.

Jesus' face and clothes were shining. His clothes were brilliant white with blazing light. Then Moses and Elijah appeared. They too had a heavenly glory about them. They began to talk with Jesus about His death in Jerusalem.

Peter didn't know what to say, so he blurted out, "It's so good to be here. Let's make three booths. One will be for You, Jesus. The others will be for Moses and Elijah."

Then a bright cloud appeared and shaded them from the sun. A voice spoke from the cloud, "This is My Son, My Chosen One. Listen to Him."

When they heard that, the three disciples fell down with their faces toward the ground. "Get up," Jesus said, touching them. "Don't be afraid."

The Transfiguration

So they got up and went down the mountain with Jesus. Along the way, Jesus told them to keep this a secret until He had risen from the dead.

The disciples asked, "Why do the Jewish leaders say Elijah must return before the Messiah comes?"

Jesus answered, "Elijah has come back. He was treated badly, as the prophets said he would be."

They realized that Jesus was talking about John the Baptist. He told them that He, the Messiah, would also suffer.

Matthew 17:1-13; Mark 9:2-13; Luke 9:28-36

*H*ere are some things Jesus said about sheep and shepherds.

"Sheep go into a sheepfold through the gate. Thieves and robbers climb over the fences. The sheep know their shepherd's voice. He speaks their names and they follow him. The sheep won't follow a stranger. They don't know the stranger's voice and will run from it."

The people listening to Jesus didn't understand what He meant. So Jesus told them about Himself, the Good Shepherd.

"I am the gate for the sheep. Many came before Me, but they were thieves and robbers. The true sheep did not listen to them. Sheep who come through Me, the gate, will be saved and will find green pastures. A thief comes to rob, kill, and destroy. I come to give life to the fullest.

Jesus the Good Shepherd

"I will give My life for My sheep. I am not like a hired man who runs away and lets wolves destroy the sheep. I will give My life willingly. No one really takes it from Me. But I will receive it again. God the Father commanded Me to do this.

"I know My sheep and they know Me. I have other sheep that are not in this flock. I must bring them all together. There will be one flock, and I will be their Shepherd."

Some people who heard Jesus thought He was crazy or had a demon. "Don't listen to Him," they said.

But others said, "A demon can't open the eyes of the blind. We have seen Jesus do that."

John 10:1-21

Jesus chose seventy-two followers for a special work. He sent them in pairs to the towns where He would come later.

"There is so much to harvest and so few workers to do it," He told them. "Don't take money; don't even take extra shoes. Don't linger along the way. Stay in one home in each village and get your food there. Bless a home when you enter it. Heal people. Tell them that God's kingdom is near.

"If a town rejects you, leave it. Cities like Tyre, Sidon, Sodom, Chorazin, Capernaum, and Bethsaida will be punished, because they saw My miracles and rejected Me. Those who welcome you are really welcoming Me. Those who reject Me are rejecting God, who sent Me."

Jesus Sends Seventy-two Helpers

When the seventy-two came back they were joyful. "We even cast out demons in Your name," they said.

Jesus answered, "I saw Satan fall from heaven. I have given you great power over the enemy. Be joyful today because your names are written in heaven."

Then Jesus was filled with the Holy Spirit. "I praise You, Father, Lord of Heaven," He said. "You have hidden these truths from smart people. But You have let these ordinary people see them."

Jesus also said, "The Father and I know each other. I choose to tell others about the Father so they can know Him. You are blessed to see what you have seen. Many prophets and kings wished they could see the things that you have seen."

Luke 10:1-24

Jesus and His disciples were on their way to Jerusalem.

Along the way they came to the village of Bethany, where Mary and Martha lived with their brother, Lazarus. They invited Jesus for dinner.

Martha worked frantically to get dinner ready, while Mary sat listening to everything Jesus said.

Jesus Visits Mary and Martha

Martha didn't like this, and she complained to Jesus. "Mary is just sitting here while I do all the work. Tell her to come and help me."

"Martha, Martha," Jesus said. "You are worried and concerned about so many things. But only one thing is really worth the concern you are showing. Mary has chosen the best. I won't take that from her."

Luke 10:38-42

One day when Jesus had finished praying, one of His disciples asked Him, "Will You teach us how to pray, as John taught his disciples?"

So this was the prayer that Jesus taught. "Father, help us to honor Your name. Send Your kingdom here on earth. Give us our food each day. Forgive our sins, as we forgive others who sin against us. Please protect us from temptation."

Jesus Teaches His Disciples How to Pray

Then Jesus told a story to help them understand prayer better. "Suppose a friend comes for a surprise visit in the middle of the night. So you go to your next-door neighbor and tell him your problem. 'A friend has just come to my home and I have no food to give him.' At first this neighbor might tell you to go away. But if you keep on knocking at his door, he will give you what you want.

"That's the way prayer is. Keep on asking. Keep on knocking. The door will be opened. Whoever asks will receive. Whoever seeks will find. Whoever knocks will get answers."

Then Jesus talked to the fathers. "If your son asks for bread, will you give him a rock? If he asks for fish, will you give him a scorpion? You know how to give good gifts to your children. So your Heavenly Father will give the Holy Spirit when you ask."

Luke 11:1-13

When Lazarus of Bethany got sick, his sisters Mary and Martha sent someone to tell Jesus to come. But Jesus stayed where He was two more days.

"Now let's go," He said to His disciples. Jesus loved Mary, Martha, and Lazarus, so He was not being unkind to them. He wanted to show them His great miracle-working power. "Lazarus is asleep," Jesus said. "I must go to wake him."

"If he's asleep, he will get well," the disciples said. But Jesus meant that Lazarus had died.

"I'm glad I wasn't there to heal him. Now you will see something to help you believe in Me."

When Martha heard that Jesus had arrived, she ran to meet Him.

Jesus Raises Lazarus from the Dead

"If only You had been here," she said, "Lazarus would not have died. But God will still hear You. It's not too late." Martha was saying that Lazarus would rise on the resurrection day. "I am the resurrection and the life," Jesus said.

Lazarus had been buried in a tomb for four days, but Jesus told them to roll the stone from the entrance. Everyone gathered around to watch, including some religious leaders who had come to comfort Mary and Martha.

"Lazarus, come out!" Jesus shouted. Lazarus walked from the tomb, wrapped in his graveclothes. Jesus had raised him from the dead.

Now the religious leaders wanted to kill Jesus. They knew people would follow Him instead of them.

John 11:1-44

Jesus and His disciples were on a trip to Jerusalem, traveling along the border between Samaria and Galilee. As they came into a village, ten lepers cried out to Jesus.

"Help us!" they begged. But they stayed at a distance, as lepers were supposed to do.

"Go to a priest," Jesus said. "Show him that you are healed." As they ran to find the priest, their leprosy went away. They were healed.

Jesus Heals Ten Lepers

One man, a Samaritan, came back to Jesus and fell down before Him with his face in the dust. He praised God and thanked Jesus for healing him.

"But I healed ten men," Jesus said. "Where are the other nine? Is this Samaritan man the only one to give glory to God?"

Then Jesus spoke to the man. "Stand up," He said. "You may go now. Your faith has healed you."

Luke 17:11-19

Have you ever wondered if Jesus cares about children?
Does He love them? This story from the Gospels tells
us the answer.

Some mothers brought their children to Jesus so He could
bless them. The disciples thought Jesus was too busy, or maybe
they thought He was too important for little children.
So they told the mothers to go away.

Jesus and the Children

But Jesus saw what the disciples were doing, and He was not happy about it. Jesus said to the disciples, "Let the children come to Me. Don't stop them! The kingdom of God is filled with trusting, childlike people. Anyone who comes to God must come like a little child. A person who doesn't do that cannot get into God's kingdom."

Jesus lifted the children into His arms. He put His hands on them and blessed them. Clearly, Jesus loves all the children of the world.

Matthew 19:13-15; Mark 10:13-16; Luke 18:15-17

Zaccheus lived in the village of Jericho, where he was a leader of the tax collectors. The Jewish people hated tax collectors, because they collected money from their own people to give to the Roman government. But this work had made Zaccheus very rich.

Zaccheus heard that Jesus was coming to Jericho, and he wanted to see Him. But he was a short man, so he could not see over the many people crowded around Jesus.

Then Zaccheus had an idea. He ran ahead of the crowd and climbed up into a sycamore tree. Now he could see Jesus when He passed by.

When Jesus saw Zaccheus in the tree He spoke to him. "Zaccheus, come down. I want to come to your house today."

Zaccheus was surprised,

Jesus Gives Zaccheus a New Life

and so was everyone else, that Jesus was going to visit a hated tax collector. Some people even began to complain.

"Jesus is going to the house of a terrible sinner," they grumbled.

But Zacchaeus came down fast and took Jesus home with him.

"Lord, from now on I will give half of all I own to the poor," Zacchaeus said to Jesus. "If I have cheated someone on his taxes, I will give back four times as much as I took."

"Salvation has come to your house today," Jesus said. "You are Jewish, but a lost person. But I, the Messiah, have come to find and save lost people."

Luke 19:1-10

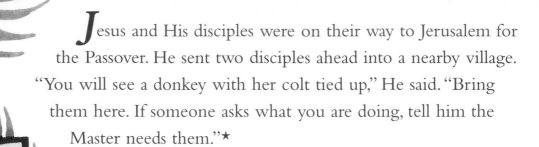

Jesus and His disciples were on their way to Jerusalem for the Passover. He sent two disciples ahead into a nearby village. "You will see a donkey with her colt tied up," He said. "Bring them here. If someone asks what you are doing, tell him the Master needs them."★

The two disciples brought the animals to Jesus. They put their cloaks over the colt so Jesus could ride on it. Some people threw their cloaks on the path where Jesus would ride. Others cut tree branches and put them on the ground ahead of Him.

The crowds swarmed around Jesus. "Praise to the Son of David," they shouted. "Praise to the One who comes in the

The Triumphal Entry

Palm Sunday

name of the Lord." Soon the whole city of Jerusalem was stirred up with this celebration.

"Who's coming?" some asked. "Jesus, the prophet from Galilee," said others. "He is the One who speaks for God."

At last Jesus came into Jerusalem. He chased the merchants and moneychangers out of the temple again. "My house is a house of worship," Jesus told them. "You have made it a place of thieves." He healed blind and crippled people in the temple.

All of this made the religious leaders angry. Once again they were jealous and afraid that people would follow Jesus instead of them. "Don't you hear the children?" they demanded. "They're shouting, 'Praise to the Son of David!' "

"Of course I hear them," Jesus answered. "But don't you remember the Scriptures? They say that even little children will honor Me."

*This fulfilled an Old Testament prophecy, "Tell Jerusalem that her King is coming. He is gentle, riding on a donkey's colt" (Zechariah 9:9; Isaiah 62:11).

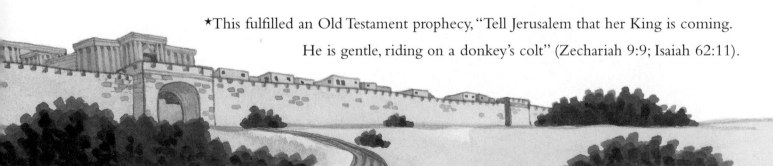

Matt. 21:1-11; Mark 11:1-11; Luke 19:28-44; John 12:12-19

The religious leaders were jealous and angry because crowds of people were following Jesus. Even little children were praising Him. The leaders wanted to find some way to trap Jesus by getting Him to say something wrong.

They sent some of their men to ask Jesus a trick question. "You're an honest man," they said. "We know that You always tell the truth. So tell us this: should we pay taxes to Caesar or shouldn't we?"

Jesus seemed trapped. If He said they should not pay taxes, the Romans would be angry with Him. If He said they should pay taxes, the Jewish people would be angry with Him. What should He say?

Jesus Talks about Caesar and God

Tuesday

1

"You evil people," Jesus said. "Why are you trying to trap Me? But I will answer you when you show Me a coin."

So they handed a Roman coin to Jesus. "Whose picture and name are on this coin?" Jesus asked.

"Caesar's," they said. Caesar was the emperor of the Roman empire.

"Well, if this is Caesar's, give it to him," Jesus said. "But make sure you give God what belongs to Him."

The religious leaders were amazed at Jesus' answer. What more could they say?

Matthew 22:15-22; Mark 12:13-17; Luke 20:20-26

In the temple were little collection boxes. People dropped their offerings for God's house into these boxes.

One day Jesus was standing at the temple watching people do this. Rich people came and put in lots of money in a showy manner. They wanted people to see them and praise them for their large gifts.

Then a poor widow came up to a collection box and dropped in two small coins. The coins were not worth much. Certainly the rich people had given much, much more than she had.

The Widow's Little Coin

But Jesus said, "Look at that poor widow. She has given much more than all the rich people together. They gave a small part of what they did not need, but she gave most of what she did need."

The disciples learned a great lesson about giving from Jesus. Perhaps we can also learn that great lesson.

Mark 12:41-44; Luke 21:1-4

*E*ach year Jewish people came to Jerusalem from all parts of the world to celebrate Passover, recalling the night when the Israelites were freed from slavery in Egypt.

The feast celebrated the "passing over." That's when the angel passed over Israelite homes with lamb's blood around the doorways. In homes that were not passed over, the oldest son died that night.

Judas Bargains for Jesus

Tuesday

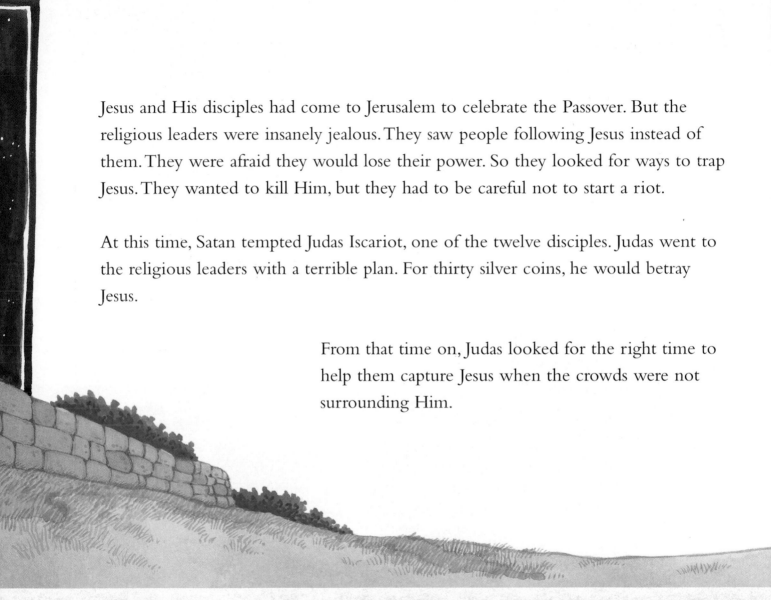

Jesus and His disciples had come to Jerusalem to celebrate the Passover. But the religious leaders were insanely jealous. They saw people following Jesus instead of them. They were afraid they would lose their power. So they looked for ways to trap Jesus. They wanted to kill Him, but they had to be careful not to start a riot.

At this time, Satan tempted Judas Iscariot, one of the twelve disciples. Judas went to the religious leaders with a terrible plan. For thirty silver coins, he would betray Jesus.

From that time on, Judas looked for the right time to help them capture Jesus when the crowds were not surrounding Him.

Matthew 26:14-16; Mark 14:10-11; Luke 22:3-6

Jesus sent two disciples into Jerusalem to get the Passover supper ready. "You will meet a man carrying a jar of water," He told them. "Follow him. Tell the master of his house that I have sent you to see the upstairs room he has ready. Prepare the supper there."

When the disciples went into Jerusalem, everything was the way He had said. That evening, Jesus and the other disciples went to the room for supper. They lay back on benches around the table, the way people did in those days.

"One of you is going to betray Me," Jesus said. The disciples were very sad to hear that. "I'm not the one, am I?" they began to ask. When Judas asked, Jesus whispered back, "Yes, you are the betrayer."

The Last Supper

"It is one of you eating with Me at this very moment," Jesus said to the others. "I must die, as the prophets said. But it would be better for My betrayer if he had never been born."

Then Jesus took bread and thanked God for it, and gave it to the disciples. "This bread is My body," He said. "Eat it!" Then He took wine and thanked God for it. "This is My blood, which seals the New Covenant. It is poured out to forgive the sins of many. Drink it!"

Jesus told the disciples, "You will all desert Me tonight." But Peter said, "Never!"

Jesus looked at him. "Tonight you will deny Me three times."

When supper was over, they sang a hymn, then they went together to the Mount of Olives.

Matt. 26:17-30; Mark 14:12-26; Luke 22:7-34; John 13:1-38

After they ate, Jesus led His disciples to a lovely grove of olive trees on the Mount of Olives, called Gethsemane. There Jesus said, "Stay here while I go pray. But you must pray too, that you will resist temptation."

He took Peter, James, and John a few feet away. "I am so weighed down with sorrow that it seems like I will die," Jesus told them. "Stay awake with Me while I go over there to pray."

Jesus knelt with His face to the ground. "Father, if You are willing, take this horrible time away from Me," He prayed. "But I want Your will to be done." An angel came from heaven to give Him strength. Jesus was so crushed with sadness that He sweat great drops of blood.

Jesus Prays in Gethsemane

When Jesus went back to the three disciples, they were asleep. "Peter, couldn't you stay awake with Me an hour?" Jesus asked. "Wake up! Pray! You need strength to resist temptation. You really want to do what is right, but your body is weak."

Jesus left the three disciples again to pray. "Father, if there is no other way except for Me to suffer, I will do it," He prayed. A second and third time Jesus came back to the three, and each time found them sleeping.

"You can't sleep now," He said. "Get up! Here comes the one who will betray Me."

Matt. 26:36-46; Mark 14:32-42; Luke 22:39-46; John 18:1

A crowd swarmed into the Garden of Gethsemane, where Jesus and His disciples had come to pray (or sleep, in the case of the disciples). But there was no time now for sleep or prayer. The crowd carried torches and swords and clubs too.

Judas had told the leaders to arrest the one he greeted. He rushed over to Jesus, hugged Him, and kissed Him on the cheek.

"Judas, are you betraying Me with a kiss?" Jesus asked him. Then he said to the men, "Whom are you looking for?"

"Jesus of Nazareth," the leaders answered.

"I am Jesus," He said. "Now let my friends go."

Judas Betrays Jesus

Thursday

The crowd backed up and fell to the ground. They were afraid of Him. But Peter pulled out a sword and swung it at Malchus, a servant of the high priest, and cut off his right ear.

"Put that sword away, Peter," Jesus said. "You could get hurt. Don't you know that I could pray, and thousands of angels would rescue Me? But how would the Scriptures be fulfilled then?" Jesus touched Malchus' ear, and it was healed.

He turned to the crowd. "Am I a dangerous criminal, that you bring swords and clubs to arrest Me? I was with you in the temple. You didn't try to arrest Me then."

Then the disciples all ran away. Mark tried to follow Jesus at a distance, but the mob tore off his clothing. They took Jesus to Jerusalem. What happened to Judas? He felt so guilty that he hanged himself.

Matt. 26:47-56; Mark 14:43-52; Luke 22:47-53; John 18:2-11

Jesus was arrested by police and soldiers. They took Him to the home of Caiaphas, the high priest. The entire religious "supreme court" came together there to try to find something wrong with Jesus so they could put Him to death.

Some people told lies about Him. But the liars didn't agree with each other. "He said He could rebuild the temple in three days," someone said.

Jesus Is Taken before the Leaders

Thursday

"Well, what do You say about that?" the high priest shouted at Jesus. But Jesus would not answer.

"Are you the Messiah?" the high priest asked Jesus.

"Yes," said Jesus. "You will see Me someday at God's right hand. I will come back to earth someday among the clouds of heaven."

The high priest tore his clothing. "Blasphemy!" he shouted. "We don't need witnesses."

So the other leaders joined the high priest, crying out for Jesus to die. Some even spat at Him. They blindfolded Him, then hit His face and laughed. "Who hit You? Tell us, prophet," they taunted. Then the guards led Jesus away and beat Him.

Matt. 26:57-68; Mark 14:53-65; Luke 22:63-71; John 18:12-40

Peter had followed the mob from Gethsemane at a distance. He went into the courtyard of the high priest's home, where the soldiers had built a fire to keep warm. Peter came near the fire, and a girl who worked for the high priest saw him. "You were with Jesus, weren't you?" she said. "No! I don't know what you're talking about," Peter answered.

Later another servant saw Peter standing by the gate. "You're one of Jesus' followers," she said. "I don't even know the man!" Peter answered. He even swore that he did not know Jesus.

Still later some others came to Peter. "You're one of Jesus' disciples. We're sure of it," they said. One of them was a relative of

Peter Denies that He Knows Jesus

Malchus, whose ear Peter had cut off in Gethsemane. Then Peter began to curse. "I don't know what you're talking about," he said. Just then a rooster crowed.

At that very moment Jesus was led past Peter. When the rooster crowed, Jesus turned to look at him. Peter remembered what Jesus had told him the night before: "Before the rooster crows, you will deny me three times." Then Peter ran out of the courtyard and cried and cried.

Matt. 26:69-75; Mark 14:66-72; Luke 22:54-62; John 18:15-27

At the trial, the religious leaders accused Jesus of blasphemy because He said He was the Messiah. They wanted to kill Him, but only the Roman rulers were allowed to put criminals to death. So in the early morning hours, they sent Jesus to Pilate, the Roman governor.

"What has He done wrong?" Pilate asked. "He has started riots," they said, and accused Jesus of many crimes. Jesus would not answer their charges, and this surprised Pilate.

"Are You the King of the Jews?" he asked. "I am not an earthly king," Jesus said. "But I am a king. People who know the truth follow Me." Then Pilate asked, "But what is truth?"

When Pilate heard that Jesus was from Galilee, he sent Him to Herod Antipas, who ruled there. When Jesus refused to do a miracle for him, Herod made fun of Him. He put a royal robe on Jesus and sent Him back to Pilate.

Each year the Romans would free one Jewish prisoner. "I will set Jesus free," Pilate told the religious leaders.

Jesus Goes before Pilate and Herod

Friday

"No, give us Barabbas," they shouted. Barabbas was a well-known criminal.

"Then what should I do with Jesus?" Pilate asked. "Crucify Him!" the leaders shouted. By this time they had a mob shouting with them.

Now Pilate was afraid. His wife wanted him to set Jesus free. "I had a terrible dream last night about all of this," she said. But Pilate was also afraid of starting a riot, because then he would be in trouble with the emperor. So he set Barabbas free and sent Jesus to be crucified.

Matt. 27:11-26; Mark 15:1-15; Luke 23:1-25; John 18:28—19:16

The Roman soldiers could be quite cruel. They made fun of Jesus by putting a royal robe on Him and putting a crown of thorns on His head. They beat Jesus and spat on Him. They bowed down and pretended to worship Him.

At last they were bored with all of this. So they took the royal robe from Jesus and put His own clothes back on Him. Then they led Him away to be crucified.

A man named Simon of Cyrene had just arrived from the country. When Jesus could not carry His cross anymore, the soldiers forced Simon to carry it.

Jesus Is Beaten and Sent to the Cross   Friday

Crowds swarmed around the procession. Women cried for Jesus, but He told them not to cry for Him. He said that the time would come when terrible things would happen to Jerusalem. People would wish they could die.

Two criminals were also being led away to be crucified.

The whole procession came to a hill just outside the city wall. This hill was called Golgotha, or "The Skull," because that is what it looked like. There Jesus and the two criminals would be crucified.

Matt. 27:27-34; Mark 15:16-23; Luke 23:26-31; John 19:17-25

Around 9 o'clock in the morning, the soldiers nailed Jesus and the two criminals to crosses and set them in the ground, with Jesus in the middle. Pilate had a sign put above Jesus that said, "Jesus, King of the Jews."

The religious leaders complained to Pilate. "Change it," they said. "Make it read 'He said He was king of the Jews.'"

But Pilate would not do it. "What I have written stays written," he said.

The soldiers divided Jesus' clothing and threw dice to see who would have His robe.

Jesus Is Crucified

A.D. 30   Good Friday

Many people came by and made fun of Jesus. "Come down from the cross and we will believe in You," they mocked. At first, both criminals joined in. Then one begged for forgiveness.

Jesus saw His mother, Mary, with John. He told John to take care of her.

At 3 that afternoon, Jesus cried out to God. Just before He died, He called out, "It is finished!" At that moment, the sky grew dark, the temple curtain tore apart, the earth shook, rocks broke, and dead people came back to life. Even the Roman soldiers were afraid. Now some of them knew that Jesus was God's Son.

Jesus was crucified because it was part of God's plan of salvation. He died on the cross for you and me, making it possible for us to have our sins forgiven. But we must ask Jesus to do that for us. Perhaps you would like to do that now.

Matt. 27:35-56; Mark 15:22-41; Luke 23:32-49; John 19:18-37

*T*he religious leaders asked Pilate to break the legs of the three men to make them die faster, so they could be taken from the crosses before the Sabbath began. Jesus was already dead, so the Roman soldiers did not break His legs. But one of them cut deep into His side with a spear. Blood and water came out. The Old Testament Scriptures had said that things would happen this way.

Late that afternoon, a rich man named Joseph from a town called Arimathea asked Pilate for Jesus' body. Nicodemus, the religious leader who had once come to see Jesus at night, helped Joseph.

The two men wrapped Jesus' body in a long linen cloth, with an ointment of myrrh and aloes that

Jesus Is Buried

Friday

Nicodemus had brought mixed into the cloth. This was the way Jews prepared a body for burial. The two men laid Jesus' body in Joseph's own tomb. Then they rolled a great round stone across the opening.

Meanwhile the religious leaders went back to Pilate. "That man said He would come back from the dead within three days," they said. "Put guards around the tomb so His followers can't steal His body and say He came back to life."

Pilate told them, "Use your own temple police." So they did. They put their guards there and sealed the tomb so no one could get at it.

Matt. 27:57-66; Mark 15:42-47; Luke 23:50-56; John 19:31-42

When the Sabbath ended Saturday evening, Mary and Mary Magdalene bought spices. It was still dark on Sunday morning when they went to Jesus' tomb to put them on His body.

Suddenly there was a great earthquake. An angel of the Lord rolled the great stone from the entrance. His face shone like lightning, and his clothes were brilliant white. When the guards saw him, they were terrified and fainted.

The women went into the tomb, where they saw another angel sitting near the place where Jesus had been. "Don't be afraid," the angel said. "You are looking for Jesus, but He isn't here. He has come back to life again, as He said He would. Now go and tell the other disciples that Jesus has risen from the dead and will meet them in Galilee."

Jesus' Followers Visit His Tomb

Easter Sunday

1

So the women rushed off. The disciples could not believe their story. It seemed like a fairy tale. But Peter and John ran to the tomb to see for themselves.

Meanwhile, Mary Magdalene had gone back to the tomb, where she was weeping. "Why are you crying?" two angels asked. "Because they have taken My Lord away," she answered. "I don't know where to find Him." As Mary looked over her shoulder, she saw someone and thought it must be the gardener. "Tell me where you have put Him," Mary begged.

"Mary!" Jesus said. For it was Jesus. "Master!" Mary answered. Then she rushed back to tell the other disciples. When Peter and John came to the tomb, they saw the linen cloth that had been wrapped around Jesus. It was folded neatly. Now Peter and John believed that Jesus had risen from the dead.

Meanwhile the temple police told the religious leaders what had happened. The leaders had a big meeting and gave the police some money to say they had fallen asleep and Jesus' disciples stole His body. So the guards took the money and lied about Jesus. Many people believed them.

Matt. 28:1-15; Mark 16:1-11; Luke 24:1-12; John 20:1-18

Later that same day two disciples were going to Emmaus, a town about seven miles west of Jerusalem. As they walked and talked, another man was suddenly there with them.

"Why are you so worried?" he asked.

Cleopas answered, "Terrible things have happened this week. Haven't you heard?"

"What things?" the man asked.

"The Prophet Jesus, a great teacher, did many miracles," they said. "We had hoped He was the Messiah. But the religious leaders had Him arrested. They crucified Him! Some of our women went to His tomb yesterday, and they said they saw angels. His body is missing!"

"Foolish people," their fellow traveler said. "Is it so hard to believe what the prophets said in

On the Road to Emmaus

the Scriptures? They told how the Messiah must suffer before going into His glory." Then he taught these two men from the Scriptures that we now call the Old Testament.

When they arrived in Emmaus, the two asked him to eat with them. When they were ready to eat, the stranger thanked God for the bread, then broke it and gave it to them. Suddenly the men realized that their fellow traveler was Jesus! But at that very moment, He was gone. "Didn't our hearts feel strangely warm when He was with us?" they said. Then they rushed back to Jerusalem and found the eleven disciples.

The disciples said, "The Lord is risen! Peter has seen Him."

Then the two men from Emmaus told their story. Now the disciples knew for sure that Jesus had risen from the dead.

Mark 16:12-13; Luke 24:13-35

That same evening the disciples were meeting secretly, because they were still afraid of the religious leaders. Suddenly Jesus was with them. They thought He was a ghost.

"Why are you afraid?" Jesus asked. "Touch Me! Be sure that I am not a ghost." He showed them the wounds in His hands and feet. Now the disciples had both joy and doubt. They didn't know what to believe.

"Do you remember what I told you earlier?" Jesus asked. "It was written in the Scriptures that the Messiah must suffer and die, and rise from the dead on the third day. You have seen these prophecies actually happen.

Jesus Appears to His Disciples

"The Scriptures also said that this Good News must be taken to all nations. Those who turn to Me will be forgiven. Later I will send the Holy Spirit on you, as the Father promised. Stay in Jerusalem until He comes and fills you with power from heaven."

One of the disciples, Thomas, was not at that meeting, so he didn't believe Jesus had really been there. "I won't believe until I can put my fingers into the wounds in His hands," he said.

Eight days later the disciples were together when Jesus appeared again. "Put your finger into My hands," Jesus said to Thomas. "Don't be filled with doubts any more."

"My Lord and My God," Thomas said. "You believe Me because you have seen Me," Jesus said. "But blessed are people who have not seen Me and still believe."

Mark 16:14; Luke 24:36-40; John 20:19-31

Jesus appeared to His disciples several times after that. Once, several of the disciples were fishing on the Sea of Galilee. They fished all night and caught nothing.

In the morning they saw a man standing on the beach. "Did you catch anything?" he asked.

"Not a thing," they replied. "Throw your net over the right side," he called to them. When they did, they could hardly bring in all the fish.

"It's the Lord!" John said to Peter. So Peter jumped into the water and swam to shore.

When the disciples got to shore, they found Jesus cooking fish and bread over a fire.

After breakfast, Jesus said to Peter, "Do you love Me more than the others do?"

"Yes," said Peter. "Feed My lambs," Jesus said.

Catching Fish with Jesus

Then Jesus asked a second and third time, "Peter, do you love Me?" Peter felt sad that Jesus would ask him this. "You know that I love You, Lord," Peter answered.

"Feed My sheep," Jesus said. "When you were little, you could go anywhere you wanted. But when you grow old, you will stretch out your hands. Others will take you where you don't want to go." Jesus was telling Peter that he also would be crucified. But he would bring glory to God.

Then Jesus said to Peter, "Follow Me." When Peter turned around, he saw John. "What about him?" Peter asked. "If I want John to live until I come back to earth, why should you care?" Jesus answered.

A rumor began among the disciples that John would never die. But Jesus didn't say that. He merely said that Peter should not be concerned about how John would die.

John 21

On a certain day, Jesus led His disciples along the road to Bethany. There on the Mount of Olives, He gave His disciples a commandment that we call the Great Commission.

"All power on heaven and earth has been given to Me," He said. "Go and make disciples in all nations. Baptize them in the name of the Father, the Son, and the Holy Spirit. Teach them to obey all the commands I have given you. Know this for sure: I will be with you always, even until the end of the world."

Jesus lifted His hands toward heaven and blessed His followers. Then He ascended into the sky and on into heaven.

Jesus Ascends into Heaven

The disciples just stood there and stared.

Suddenly two angels in white robes appeared. "Why are you staring into the sky?" they asked. "Jesus has gone back to heaven. But someday He will come back here, as He left."

Then the disciples walked the half-mile back to Jerusalem. They were filled with great joy.

Matt. 28:16-20; Mark 16:15-20; Luke 24:50-53; Acts 1:1-11

*B*ack in Jerusalem, 120 of Jesus' followers spent a lot of time together, including Peter, John, James, Andrew, Philip, Thomas, Bartholomew, Matthew, James the son of Alphaeus, Simon the Zealot, Judas son of James, the brothers of Jesus, and several women including Mary. They praised God and had long prayer meetings.

At one of their meetings, Peter made a suggestion. "Judas was one of us twelve disciples," he said. "We should choose another person to take his place. This person must also be a witness of Jesus' resurrection. He must have seen everything we have seen about the risen Christ."

The group suggested two men, Joseph Justus, also called Barsabbas, and Matthias. The disciples prayed for the right person to be chosen, then they "cast lots."

The Disciples Wait in an Upstairs Room

(It was something like drawing straws.) God did guide them, and Matthias was chosen as the new twelfth disciple.

Seven weeks had gone by since Jesus' death and resurrection. One day when the disciples were meeting in the upstairs room, they heard a roaring sound, like a great wind. Little flames of fire came upon each person's head. Everyone in the room was filled with the Holy Spirit and spoke languages they never knew.

Many godly Jews from other countries were in Jerusalem for a festival called Pentecost. When they heard the disciples speaking in the languages of their countries, they were amazed.

Then Peter told the people about Jesus the Messiah. He begged them to accept Jesus as their Savior. That day 3,000 people believed and were baptized.

Acts 1:12–2:41

As Peter and John went to the temple one afternoon, they saw a man who was crippled from birth. The man saw them too, and begged for money.

"Look," Peter said to him. "We have no money to give you, but we have something better. In the name of Jesus, get up and walk." Peter lifted the man up, and he began jumping around, praising God.

The people recognized this lame beggar. Peter saw the crowds staring, so he began to preach. "God did this miracle to bring glory to Jesus, whom you crucified. But John and I saw Him alive after His crucifixion. Be sorry for what you have done. Turn to the Lord for forgiveness."

Some religious leaders were angry that Peter said Jesus was alive. They arrested Peter and John and put them in prison. But many who had heard Peter were sorry. They became true believers in Jesus.

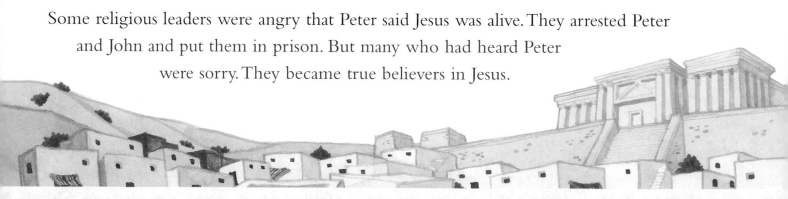

Peter and John Work a Miracle

Now there were about 5,000 people in Jerusalem who believed in Jesus as the Messiah.

The next morning Peter and John were brought before the religious council. "How did you do this miracle?" they demanded. "Who gave you the power?" Then Peter was filled with the Holy Spirit. "Jesus gave us the power," he said. "You crucified Jesus, but God has raised Him from the dead."

The leaders warned Peter and John to stop preaching, but Peter answered, "We must obey God, not you."

Peter and John told the other disciples what had happened. They all prayed for courage to preach as they should. Then the building shook, and they were all filled with the Holy Spirit. Now they were ready to do more great things for Jesus.

Acts 3:1–4:31

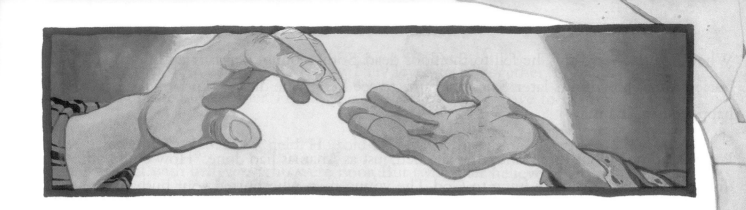

*T*he twelve apostles taught in the temple and worked many miracles. People carried the sick into the streets, hoping they would be healed. Many people were becoming believers.

The religious leaders grew even more jealous. They arrested the apostles and put them in jail, but an angel opened the jail and let them out. "Go back to the temple and preach about Jesus," the angel said. So as soon as it was daybreak, they obeyed.

Meanwhile the high priest sent guards to the jail to bring the apostles before the council. But the prisoners were gone, and the jail doors were still locked. Someone then reported that the apostles were teaching in the temple. So the temple guards arrested them and brought them before the council.

The Apostles Heal the Sick

Now there were about 5,000 people in Jerusalem who believed in Jesus as the Messiah.

The next morning Peter and John were brought before the religious council. "How did you do this miracle?" they demanded. "Who gave you the power?" Then Peter was filled with the Holy Spirit. "Jesus gave us the power," he said. "You crucified Jesus, but God has raised Him from the dead."

The leaders warned Peter and John to stop preaching, but Peter answered, "We must obey God, not you."

Peter and John told the other disciples what had happened. They all prayed for courage to preach as they should. Then the building shook, and they were all filled with the Holy Spirit. Now they were ready to do more great things for Jesus.

Acts 3:1–4:31

The believers were like one big family. They loved to be together. They shared with each other. They helped each other. Those who had lots of money gave to the poor.

One believer, Barnabas, had a field. He sold it and gave the money to the apostles so they could share it with believers who were poor. But two other believers, Ananias and Sapphira, also owned some property and sold it. They brought only part of what they got for the property. This was fine, except they claimed they were giving all of the money. They had agreed to lie about this.

Peter scolded Ananias first. "This was your money," he said. "You could do anything you wanted with it. But you lied. You told us you are giving everything. You are lying not only to us, but to the Holy Spirit."

How Early Believers Worked Together

When Ananias heard this, he fell to the floor dead. Some young men carried him out and buried him. Three hours later, Sapphira came to see Peter. She did not know what had happened to Ananias.

Peter asked her about the money and she lied, just as Ananias had done. "How could you do this?" Peter asked. "You are lying to God. The young men who buried your husband are waiting to bury you too."

Immediately Sapphira fell down and died. The young men carried her out and buried her.

Now a wave of fear swept through the believers. It became clear that God would not let His people lie to Him.

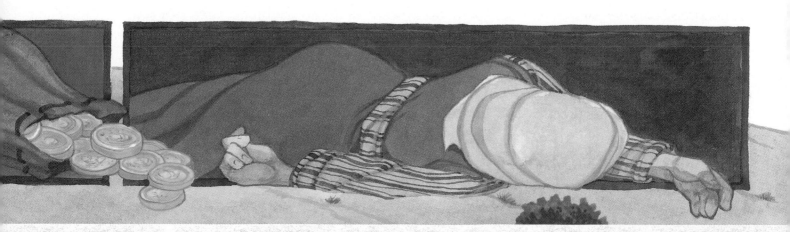

Acts 4:32–5:11

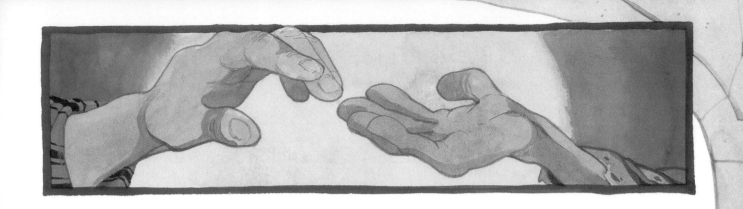

*T*he twelve apostles taught in the temple and worked many miracles. People carried the sick into the streets, hoping they would be healed. Many people were becoming believers.

The religious leaders grew even more jealous. They arrested the apostles and put them in jail, but an angel opened the jail and let them out. "Go back to the temple and preach about Jesus," the angel said. So as soon as it was daybreak, they obeyed.

Meanwhile the high priest sent guards to the jail to bring the apostles before the council. But the prisoners were gone, and the jail doors were still locked. Someone then reported that the apostles were teaching in the temple. So the temple guards arrested them and brought them before the council.

The Apostles Heal the Sick

"Stop teaching about Jesus. Stop blaming us for His death," the high priest said.

"We must obey God, not you," Peter and the other apostles said. "You did kill Him. But God brought Him back to life."

The council members were angry and wanted to kill the apostles. Then a man named Gamaliel spoke up. "Be careful how you do this," he said. "If these men are doing this on their own, they will fail. But what if they really are doing God's work? You don't want to fight God, do you?" The council listened to Gamaliel. They had the apostles beaten and set free.

But the apostles were glad they could suffer for Jesus. They kept on teaching, both in the temple and in the believers' homes, that Jesus was truly God's Son.

Acts 5:12-42

Many people were becoming Jesus' followers. But with more people came more problems. Some believers spoke Greek. Others spoke Aramaic. The people who spoke Greek felt there was discrimination against them. Their widows didn't get as much help as the Jewish widows who spoke Aramaic. So the twelve apostles called all the disciples together.

"We should not give up preaching to distribute food," they said. "Let's choose seven wise, respected men who are filled with God's Spirit, and put them in charge of distributing food. Then we can continue preaching and teaching."

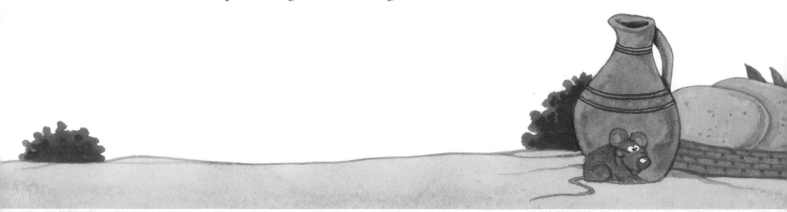

The Seven Deacons

The other disciples thought this was a good idea. They chose seven men, called deacons, to distribute food and other things. The seven included Stephen, a man filled with the Holy Spirit. There were also Philip, Prochorus, Nicanor, Timon, Parmenas, and Nicholaus, a Gentile who worshiped with the Jewish people at Antioch.

The seven were brought to the apostles, who prayed and placed their hands on them. This showed that the seven had been chosen to do God's work. The Gospel spread, and many more people in Jerusalem became believers in Jesus. Even many priests trusted in Jesus as the Messiah.

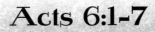

Acts 6:1-7

God gave Stephen great power to do miracles among the people. One day some members of a Jewish cult argued with him, but clearly Stephen had much greater wisdom. That's because the Holy Spirit was speaking through him. So these cult members accused Stephen of cursing Moses and God. They had him arrested and brought before the council.

"This man says Jesus will destroy the temple and change the laws that Moses gave us," they said. "Is this true?" the high priest asked.

Stephen gave a long speech to the council about the history of the Israelites. During all this, the council listened carefully. Then Stephen said, "But you betrayed and murdered Jesus, the Messiah!" Now the council members were furious. But Stephen wasn't through. He looked into heaven and said, "Heaven is opening! I see Jesus standing at God's right hand."

The council members thought this was blasphemy against God, and they covered their ears. They dragged Stephen out of the city, where they picked up large stones and stoned him. As

Stephen Is Killed

Stephen was dying, he prayed, "Lord Jesus, welcome me home. And forgive these people. They don't know what they are doing." Some godly people came and buried Stephen.

The men who were throwing rocks at Stephen had put their cloaks at the feet of a young man named Saul. This was the man who later became the great Apostle Paul. At this time, he hated Jesus' followers, and thought killing Stephen was good. From that time on, he and other leaders were very cruel to believers. They arrested many, putting both men and women into prison. Others had to leave Jerusalem.

Acts 6:8–8:3

A believer named Philip went to Samaria, where he did many miracles. Evil spirits were cast out. Paralyzed and crippled people were healed. And people listened to Philip tell the Good News about Jesus.

A sorcerer named Simon had lived there many years, amazing people with his witchcraft. When Simon heard Philip, he believed in Jesus also. He was even baptized. Then he stayed near Philip, watching his miracles.

By this time news from Samaria had gone to Jerusalem, so the apostles sent Peter and John to see what was happening. They prayed for the people there to receive the Holy Spirit.

When Simon saw this, he wanted this power. "Let me buy it from you," he said to Peter and John.

"Beg God to forgive you," said Peter. "You can't buy God's power."

Then Simon was afraid. "Pray for me!" he begged.

Philip Preaches at Samaria

Then an angel spoke to Philip. "Go to the road to Gaza," he said. Philip obeyed. While he was there he saw the treasurer of Ethiopia returning home in his chariot. He had been to Jerusalem to worship, and now he was reading a scroll of the Book of Isaiah.

"Do you understand what you are reading?" Philip asked. "No, help me," the man said. Then Philip told the man about Jesus, whom Isaiah had written about hundreds of years before.

"May I be baptized?" the Ethiopian asked. "I believe that Jesus is God's Son."

So they stopped the chariot and Philip baptized him. Then God's Spirit took Philip away to preach somewhere else, while the Ethiopian went on home, filled with joy because he was now a believer.

Acts 8:4-40

Saul was becoming more dangerous now, trying to kill Jesus' followers. He asked the high priest for letters to the religious leaders in Damascus. He wanted to arrest believers there and bring them to Jerusalem for trial.

Saul had almost reached Damascus when suddenly a brilliant light shone from heaven. Saul fell to the ground and a voice spoke to him. "Saul! Saul! Why are you hurting Me?"

"Who are You?" Saul asked. "I am Jesus, the One you are hurting," the voice answered. Now get up and go into Damascus. You will be told what to do there." The men with Saul were awestruck. They had heard the voice, but they didn't see anyone.

When Saul got up, he was blind. Someone led him into Damascus, where for three days he ate nothing and saw nothing.

Then the Lord spoke to a believer named Ananias. "Go to Judas' house on Straight Street," He said. "You will find Saul of Tarsus there. When you put your hands on him, his sight will be restored."

Saul Becomes a Believer A.D. 35

Ananias was afraid. "Lord, this man has done terrible things to believers in Jerusalem. He has come here to arrest us."

"Do what I tell you," the Lord said. "I have chosen Saul to tell many about Me. He will suffer much to do this."

So Ananias found Saul. He put his hands on him and said, "Saul, Jesus sent me. He wants you to see and to be filled with the Holy Spirit."

Suddenly Saul could see. He was baptized and stayed in Damascus, telling people that Jesus was God's Son. The believers were confused, for they knew how much he had hated them.

The Jewish religious leaders were also confused and angry. Saul was preaching about Jesus in the synagogues, telling people that Jesus really was the Messiah!

Acts 9:1-22

The religious leaders of Damascus plotted to catch Saul. They watched the city gates for him day and night, hoping to grab him and kill him.

But Saul heard about their plans. One night his new friends, the believers, let him over the wall in a big basket.

Saul returned to Jerusalem and tried to meet with the believers there, but they were afraid. They thought it was a trick.

Saul Escapes from Damascus

So Barnabas took Saul to the apostles and told them how Jesus had spoken to Saul along the road and how Saul had preached in Damascus. At last the believers accepted him.

Now Saul began to preach in Jerusalem. He told everyone he could about the Lord. He tried to speak to some of the Greek-speaking Jews, but they hated him and tried to kill him. Then the believers took Saul to Caesarea and from there to his hometown, Tarsus.

For some time, the believers in Judea, Galilee, and Samaria had peace. They worshiped the Lord. The believers grew in number. The Holy Spirit helped them in all they did.

Acts 9:23-31

Peter traveled to many places, visiting the believers. At a town called Lydda he met Aeneas, who had been paralyzed for eight years. "Aeneas, Jesus Christ has healed you," Peter said. "Get up and make your bed."

Aeneas was healed immediately. He jumped out of bed and was well. When the people of Lydda saw Aeneas walking around, they knew that a miracle had happened. So they turned to the Lord and became believers.

In the nearby city of Joppa lived a woman named Dorcas, a kind woman who gave much to help poor people. But Dorcas got sick and died. Friends washed her body and laid it in an upstairs room.

Peter Heals Aeneas and Dorcas

When the believers in Joppa heard that Peter was in Lydda, they sent two men to find him.

"Please come quickly," they told Peter. So Peter came with them to the upstairs room where many people had gathered to mourn. Widows were crying, for Dorcas had done so much for them. They showed Peter the clothes she had made for them.

Peter sent everyone from the room, then he knelt down and prayed. "Get up, Dorcas," Peter said. Dorcas opened her eyes. When she saw Peter, she sat up. Peter took her by the hand and helped her up. Then he called the believers back into the room.

The good news about Dorcas spread all over Joppa, and many believed in Jesus. Peter stayed in Joppa for some time.

Acts 9:32-43

Cornelius, the captain of a group of Roman soldiers, lived in Caesarea. He and all the people in his house worshiped God. He gave generously to the poor and prayed often.

About 3 o'clock one afternoon, Cornelius had a vision. An angel from God stood before him. Cornelius was afraid. "What do you want?" he asked.

"God has heard your prayers," said the angel. "He knows about your generous giving. Send to Joppa for a man named Peter. He is staying with Simon, a leather maker, in his house by the sea."

Cornelius sent a soldier and two servants to find Peter. Peter was up on Simon's flat rooftop, praying. He was hungry, waiting for lunch to be prepared, when he fell asleep and had a strange vision. A huge sheet descended from heaven. In it were all kinds of animals and birds that the Jews considered unclean. "Kill these and eat them," a voice said.

Peter's Vision of Unclean Animals

"Lord, these are unclean," Peter protested. "I've never eaten any unclean animal or bird." God spoke again. "When I tell you to eat it, it is not unclean."

This happened three times. Just then the three men from Cornelius arrived. "Go with them," the Holy Spirit told Peter.

So Peter and some other believers went to Caesarea to see Cornelius, who told Peter about his vision. Then Peter told Cornelius about Jesus' death and resurrection. While he spoke, the Holy Spirit came upon everyone who was listening.

It was clear now that God had given the Holy Spirit to Gentiles. The Jewish people had always thought that Gentiles were unclean. Now it was clear that God was accepting them too. So Peter gave orders for Cornelius and his family to be baptized. Then he stayed with them several days.

Acts 10

In Antioch there were many Gentiles who believed and formed a church. Paul and Barnabas stayed there a year, teaching them. They were the first believers to be called Christians.

But many believers were suffering greatly. King Herod arrested Peter and threw him into prison. But the Christians were praying for Peter.

The night before he was to be killed, he was sleeping. Suddenly an angel appeared. Peter thought he was dreaming. "Get up," the angel said. "Get dressed and follow me."

Peter's heavy chains fell off. He and the angel walked past the soldiers on either side of them and out the door. When they came to the big iron gate to the city, it opened before them.

Peter Is Put into Prison and Then Set Free

Now Peter knew that the Lord had sent this angel to rescue him.

He went to the home of Mary, John Mark's mother, where the Christians were praying for him. When he knocked on the gate, a girl named Rhoda answered. She was so excited to hear Peter's voice that she forgot to let him in! Instead she ran inside and told the others that Peter was there. They thought she was crazy.

Peter kept on knocking until someone finally opened the gate. Then Peter told them how the Lord had freed him. "Tell the other apostles what has happened," he said. Then he slipped quietly away.

The next morning Herod was furious. No one could find Peter. So Herod executed all of the men who had been Peter's guards.

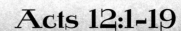

Acts 12:1-19

*T*here were several important teachers and preachers in the church at Antioch. Sometimes they went without food to show their devotion to the Lord; this is called fasting. Once when they were praying, the Holy Spirit spoke to them. "Send Saul and Barnabas to do special work for Me," He said.

The people prayed and fasted some more. Then they put their hands on Saul and Barnabas and sent them on their way to do God's work.

The Holy Spirit led them to the island of Cyprus, where a young man named John Mark joined them. (He would later write the Gospel of Mark in our Bible).

In the town of Paphos lived a false prophet named Elymas, who worked for the

Paul Begins His First Missionary Journey

governor. The governor asked Saul and Barnabas to come and talk about Jesus, but Elymas tried to stop the governor from believing.

Then Saul, who was also known now as Paul, was filled with the Holy Spirit. He said to Elymas, "You are an evil man, an enemy of all that is right. God will punish you by making you blind for a while."

Suddenly Elymas was blind. He begged others to lead him by the hand. When the governor saw that he was amazed. So he became a believer in Jesus and put his trust in Him.

Acts 13:1-12

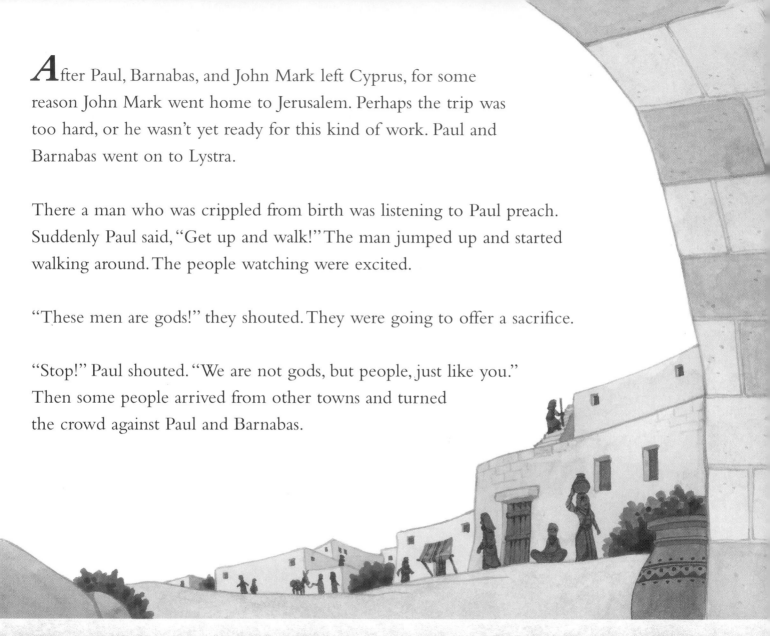

After Paul, Barnabas, and John Mark left Cyprus, for some reason John Mark went home to Jerusalem. Perhaps the trip was too hard, or he wasn't yet ready for this kind of work. Paul and Barnabas went on to Lystra.

There a man who was crippled from birth was listening to Paul preach. Suddenly Paul said, "Get up and walk!" The man jumped up and started walking around. The people watching were excited.

"These men are gods!" they shouted. They were going to offer a sacrifice.

"Stop!" Paul shouted. "We are not gods, but people, just like you." Then some people arrived from other towns and turned the crowd against Paul and Barnabas.

Some People Think Paul and Barnabas Are Gods

People began to stone Paul. Thinking he was dead, they dragged him outside the city.

Meanwhile some believers came from Judea teaching that people must first be Jews before they could be Christians. Paul and Barnabas said they were wrong, so more trouble started.

Paul and Barnabas went back to Jerusalem to meet with the apostles and other church leaders. They made a decision that all people could accept Jesus. They did not have to become Jews first.

Acts 14:1–15:21

When Paul was ready to go on a second missionary journey, Barnabas wanted to take John Mark along. Paul refused. So Barnabas took Mark and went one way, and Paul took a man named Silas and went another. They went back to see many of the people who had accepted Christ before.

Paul and Silas visited the Christians in Lystra, where a young Christian named Timothy lived. His mother, Eunice, and his grandmother, Lois, were Jewish Christians.

Timothy Becomes Paul's Helper

Timothy had a good reputation with the Christians at Lystra and Iconium, so Paul invited him to go with them.

Paul, Silas, and Timothy traveled from city to city, telling the Christians what the leaders in Jerusalem had decided about Gentiles becoming Christians. So the church grew stronger and bigger each day.

Acts 15:36–16:5; 1 & 2 Timothy

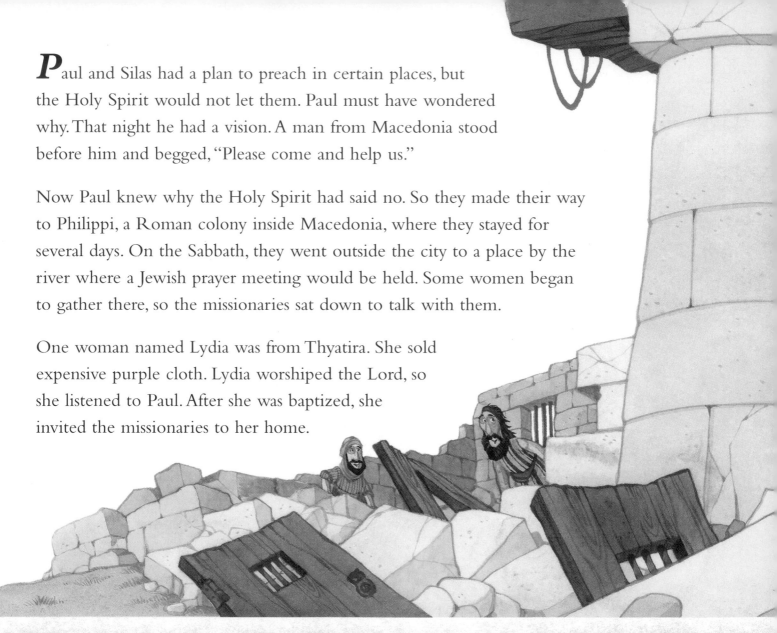

Paul and Silas had a plan to preach in certain places, but the Holy Spirit would not let them. Paul must have wondered why. That night he had a vision. A man from Macedonia stood before him and begged, "Please come and help us."

Now Paul knew why the Holy Spirit had said no. So they made their way to Philippi, a Roman colony inside Macedonia, where they stayed for several days. On the Sabbath, they went outside the city to a place by the river where a Jewish prayer meeting would be held. Some women began to gather there, so the missionaries sat down to talk with them.

One woman named Lydia was from Thyatira. She sold expensive purple cloth. Lydia worshiped the Lord, so she listened to Paul. After she was baptized, she invited the missionaries to her home.

Paul and Silas Visit Philippi

One day on the way to prayer, the missionaries saw a little slave girl with a demon in her. Paul drove the demon out, making the girl's owner angry. He had Paul and Silas thrown into jail.

At midnight Paul and Silas were singing and praising God. Suddenly the prison shook and the doors opened. The guard was terrified. Thinking that his prisoners had escaped, he started to kill himself, but Paul stopped him.

The guard cried out, "What must I do to be saved?" Paul answered, "Trust Jesus Christ!" The man and his family trusted Christ and were baptized.

The next day the city leaders realized that Paul and Silas were Roman citizens and had been put into prison without a trial. People could get into trouble for treating Roman citizens like that. So the leaders apologized and begged Paul and Silas to leave Philippi. After they said good-bye to the Christians, they were on their way.

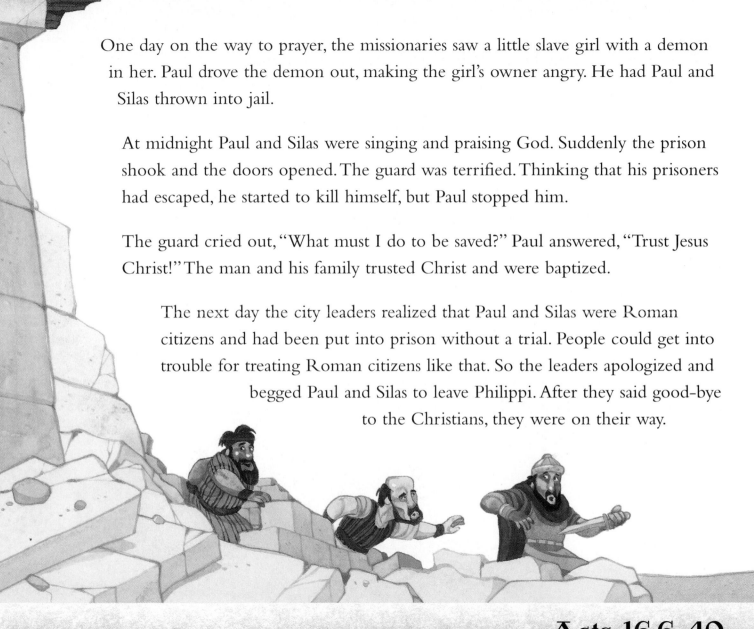

Acts 16:6-40

Wherever Paul went, he got into trouble because he said that Jesus was God's Son. In Thessalonica, many Jews were convinced that Jesus was the Messiah. But some Jewish leaders became jealous and got a mob to start a riot.

That night the Christians in Thessalonica sent Paul and his friends to Berea, where the people were more kind. They listened carefully and studied their Scriptures to see if the things Paul said were true. Many in Berea believed in Jesus.

But then the troublemakers from Thessalonica came and caused trouble in Berea. So the Christians in Berea sent Paul to the seacoast. He went all the way to Athens while Silas and Timothy stayed in Thessalonica.

In Athens, Paul preached at the Jewish meeting place and in the marketplace. Some began to argue with Paul and brought him to a Greek council. There the people

Telling Others about Jesus

listened carefully until Paul talked about Jesus' resurrection. Then some laughed. How could this be? But some of the people believed in Jesus, including a council member named Dionysius and a woman named Damaris.

From Athens, Paul went to Corinth. He met a couple named Aquila and Priscilla. They were tent-makers, which was the work Paul did to make money. So Paul stayed with them and worked with them.

Paul preached to the Jewish people, but most did not want Jesus. So Paul decided to preach to the Gentiles from that time on.

Acts 17:1–18:11

After a year and a half in Corinth, Paul went to Ephesus, visiting many other cities on the way. At each place he encouraged the Christians and helped them grow in their faith.

For more than two years Paul stayed at Ephesus, teaching about Jesus. While he was there, many people were healed. Even touching bits of Paul's clothing caused demons to leave people and helped them to be healed. Some people tried to imitate this power to heal, but they did not have the Holy Spirit in them.

Seven sons of a man named Sceva tried to drive a demon from a person, but the demon turned on them and beat them up. This brought great fear to the people in Ephesus. Soon there was a revival among the Christians. They confessed wrong things they were doing. They also brought books of witchcraft they still owned. They burned

Burning Books and a Silversmith Riot

books worth 50,000 pieces of silver. So the work of Christ became well known in Ephesus.

But there was also trouble for the Christians there. A man named Demetrius made little silver statues of the pagan goddess Diana. Demetrius and his workmen made much money from this trade, and the work of Christ in Ephesus was causing them to lose business. So Demetrius stirred up a riot against Paul. The mob rushed to the big meeting place in Ephesus.

Finally, a city leader stood before the mob. "If Demetrius knows something is wrong, he should go to our judges with it," he said. "The Romans may hurt us if we have a riot. Go home!"

The people listened. The riot was over. They all went home.

Acts 18:23–19:41

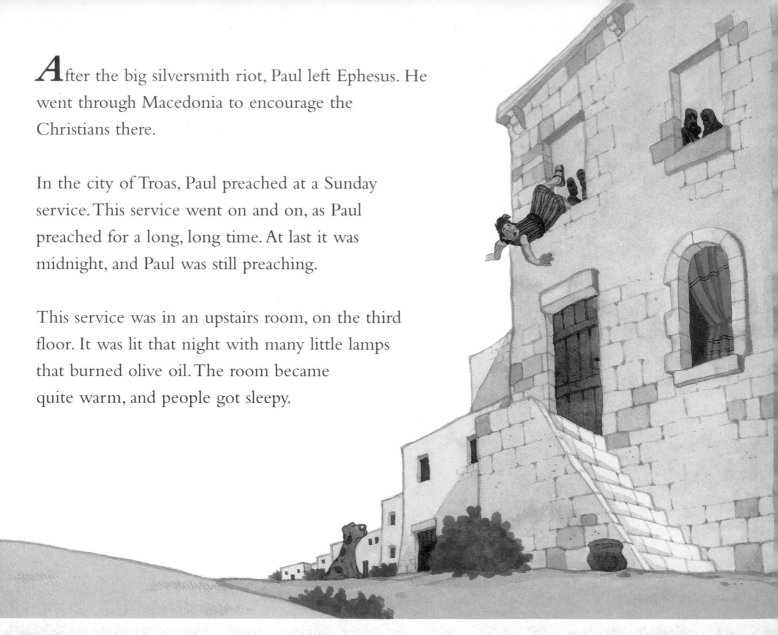

After the big silversmith riot, Paul left Ephesus. He went through Macedonia to encourage the Christians there.

In the city of Troas, Paul preached at a Sunday service. This service went on and on, as Paul preached for a long, long time. At last it was midnight, and Paul was still preaching.

This service was in an upstairs room, on the third floor. It was lit that night with many little lamps that burned olive oil. The room became quite warm, and people got sleepy.

Sleepy Eutychus

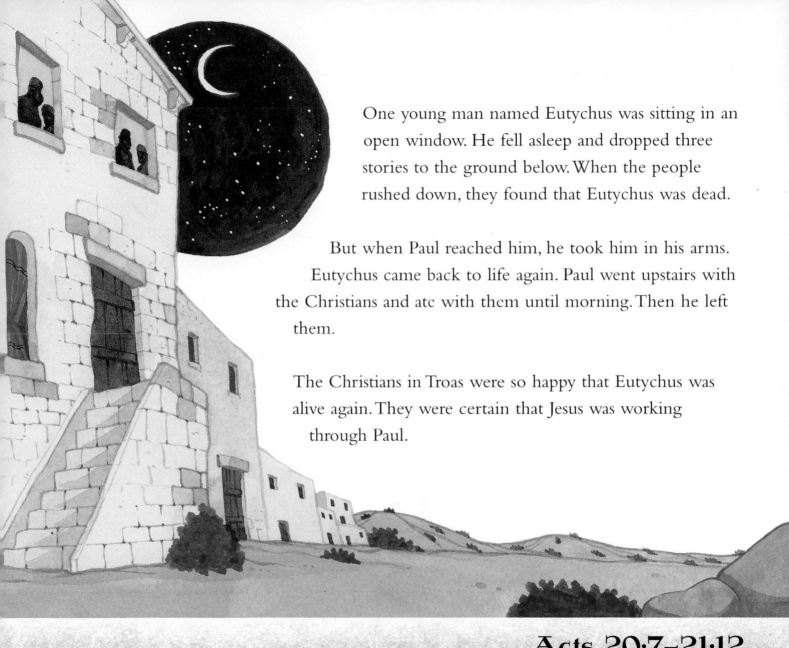

One young man named Eutychus was sitting in an open window. He fell asleep and dropped three stories to the ground below. When the people rushed down, they found that Eutychus was dead.

But when Paul reached him, he took him in his arms. Eutychus came back to life again. Paul went upstairs with the Christians and ate with them until morning. Then he left them.

The Christians in Troas were so happy that Eutychus was alive again. They were certain that Jesus was working through Paul.

Acts 20:7–21:12

Paul wanted to get back to Jerusalem in time for the festival of Pentecost. Along the way he asked the Christians at Ephesus to come to the seacoast so he could say good-bye. When they arrived, Paul told them they would never see him again. He prayed and people cried and hugged and kissed him. The same thing happened at Tyre.

Then at Caesarea, a prophet named Agabus came to see Paul. He took Paul's wide belt and tied his own hands with it. "The Holy Spirit says you will be tied up like this in Jerusalem," he said. Paul's friends begged him not to go to Jerusalem, but Paul refused to listen. "I am even willing to die for Jesus in Jerusalem," he said.

The Christians in Jerusalem welcomed Paul. Paul told them how God had used him to tell Gentiles about Jesus. The leaders told Paul about some rumors; some Jewish Christians were saying that Paul was against Jewish customs.

Paul Returns to Jerusalem

"Now here is a plan to help," they said. "Four of our men are about to shave their heads to show they follow our customs. You should do this too. Also, pay what is needed for their heads to be shaved."

So the next day Paul went with the four men for the religious ceremony at the temple. They planned to follow the ceremonies for seven days.

Acts 21:1-26

*T*oward the end of the seven days, some Jewish people from Asia stirred up a mob against Paul. "Help!" they shouted. "This man teaches against our people. He even takes Gentiles into the Temple." That wasn't true, but they had seen Paul earlier that day with Trophimus, a Gentile from Ephesus. Soon there was a riot. People dragged Paul from the temple and would have killed him, but a Roman commander stopped them. The commander brought Paul into the soldiers' headquarters.

"Let me speak to the crowd," Paul said. So the commander gave him permission. The people listened carefully as Paul spoke in Hebrew, telling them how he had become a Christian. But when he said God had sent him to Gentiles, the rioting started again.

The Roman commander did not understand what was happening. To be safe,

Paul Is Arrested at the Temple

he ordered Paul to be beaten. But Paul said, "I am a Roman citizen." The commander stopped. He could get into trouble for beating a Roman citizen without a trial.

Then he took Paul before the Jewish council. Paul told them he was a Pharisee, so the Pharisees on the council defended him. The Sadducees argued against him. Soon the council was almost in a riot. Now the commander took Paul away.

The next morning Paul's nephew heard that forty men were planning to kill Paul, so he told the Roman commander about this. The commander sent Paul that same night to Caesarea to be judged by Governor Felix.

Acts 21:27–23:31

Ananias the high priest brought a lawyer named Tertullus to Caesarea to testify against Paul. "This man is a troublemaker," Tertullus said. "He causes riots through the Roman Empire. He tells the Jews to rebel against the Roman government."

Then Governor Felix asked Paul to speak. "I have never caused riots anywhere," Paul said. "But I do believe in the way of salvation, even though I still believe in our Jewish law. These men know that I didn't start a riot. Some Jewish people from Asia came and started it. They should be here to state their case, shouldn't they?"

Several days later the governor called for Paul again. Paul told Felix and his wife, Drusilla, what it meant to be a Christian. Felix was afraid. He was not ready to become a Christian. So he sent Paul away for a while. But during the next two years, Felix listened to Paul from time to time.

Paul Goes Before the Roman Rulers

Then Festus became governor instead of Felix. He held another trial for Paul. Festus wanted to please the Jewish leaders, so he asked Paul to be tried in Jerusalem.

"No, as a Roman citizen, I want to be tried by Caesar," Paul insisted. Festus had no choice. He must now send Paul to Caesar, the Roman emperor.

Before he left for Rome, Paul was taken before King Agrippa. Paul told the king how he became a Christian. Then he said, "I wish you and others here would also become Christians."

King Agrippa talked with his advisers. They all said that Paul had done nothing to deserve prison or death. But Paul had asked for Caesar to try him, so the king had to send him to Rome.

Acts 23:33–26:32

Paul was put on a ship and sent to Italy. As the ship sailed, it began to get into rough weather. At a place called Fair Havens, the ship stopped awhile. Most ships would not sail that late in the year. Paul warned the ship's officers, "If we go on, we will likely have a shipwreck."

The captain of the ship did not agree, so they lifted anchor and set sail, keeping close to shore. A fierce wind began to blow the ship away from shore into the open sea. Finally the crew gave up and let the ship go with the wind. The seas grew higher and higher. The crew threw everything they could overboard to keep from sinking. But the storm raged for fourteen days, till at last the ship ran aground on the island of Malta. Everyone made it to shore safely.

Shipwreck!

The people of Malta were kind to the shipwrecked men. They built a fire on the beach to warm them. But as Paul was lifting some firewood, a poisonous snake bit him. The people were sure he would die. When he didn't, they decided that he must be a god.

The governor's father was sick. Paul prayed for him and healed him. Many other sick people came and Paul healed them.

At last another ship came to get them. Because Paul had helped them so much, the people of Malta gave them all they needed for the trip.

Acts 27:1–28:10

In Rome, Paul was permitted to rent a house and live in it. A soldier guarded him at all times.

Three days after he arrived, Paul had a meeting with the local Jewish leaders. He told them all that had happened. "We want to listen to you," they said. "People are talking about Christians everywhere."

So a meeting was called and Paul talked about Jesus. Some believed in Jesus. Others would not. Paul criticized the Jews who rejected Jesus. "You don't want to understand," he said. "But the Gentiles are accepting Jesus."

Paul Stays at Rome

A.D. 70 Romans destroy Jerusalem

For the next two years, Paul lived in his rented house. No one stopped him from telling visitors about Jesus. During this time he wrote letters to believers; some of these letters became books of our New Testament, like Philemon, Colossians, Ephesians, and Philippians.

The Bible does not tell us what happened next, but many people think the Emperor Nero set Paul free. He may have made another missionary journey.

Then he was sent to Rome again, this time not to a rented house, but to prison. At that time most of his friends deserted him. A tradition says that Paul's head was cut off, probably in A.D. 67 or 68. But toward the end of his life Paul wrote triumphantly, "I have finished the course. I have kept the faith."

Acts 28:11-31

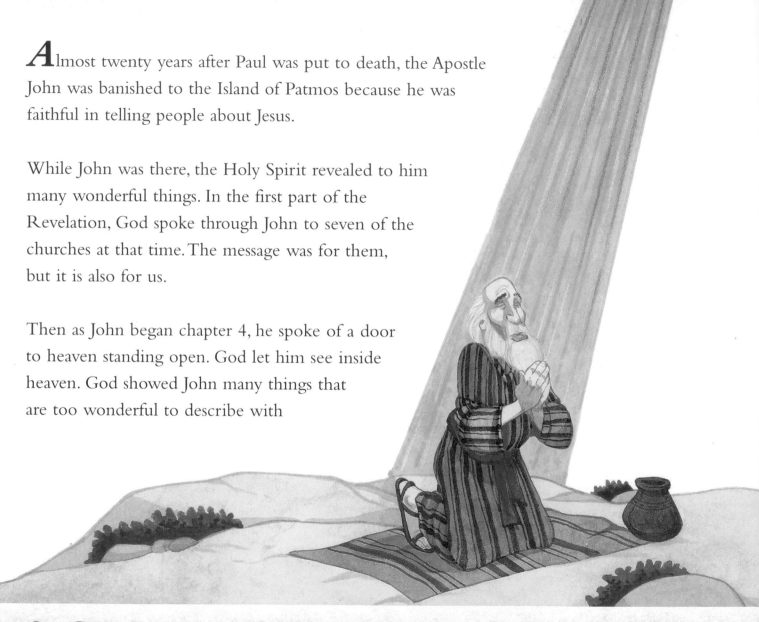

Almost twenty years after Paul was put to death, the Apostle John was banished to the Island of Patmos because he was faithful in telling people about Jesus.

While John was there, the Holy Spirit revealed to him many wonderful things. In the first part of the Revelation, God spoke through John to seven of the churches at that time. The message was for them, but it is also for us.

Then as John began chapter 4, he spoke of a door to heaven standing open. God let him see inside heaven. God showed John many things that are too wonderful to describe with

On Patmos, John Writes about the Things to Come

words, so it is hard for us to understand all of what John wrote down.

But God did make it clear that His home, heaven, is a wonderful place. There is no pain or suffering there. There is no longer death. There is no sin. Heaven is a place so beautiful that no one can really describe it. It is a place that never rusts, decays, or stops. It is there forever.

But the most important thing about heaven is the Lord Himself. He will always be there. Those of us who accept Jesus as our Savior will live with Him forever in His wonderful home.

The Book of Revelation

The story of the Bible begins with Creation. God made everything, including the world and people. The first people were Adam and Eve. But sin came into the world through Satan. His work has always been to resist God and destroy our lives. He makes sin look good and fun so we will want to do it. But sin is dark and evil, for it keeps us from walking with God.

God worked with many people through the years. The Bible story unfolds through people like Abraham, Isaac, Jacob, David, and many others. These people sinned, but they showed us that God will take our sin away and forgive us.

The Story Goes On Today

Then Jesus came. He is God's Son, the Messiah the people of Israel expected. Jesus worked miracles and changed lives. But more important, He died on the cross to save us from our sins. He rose from the dead to show us that He has power over death. He went up into heaven and is with God the Father. But He has sent the Holy Spirit to guide us.

We who live today have the Bible, God's Word. Through His Word, God shows us how to have our sins forgiven. He shows us how to walk with Him. The story of the Bible, the power of God's Word, lives on through you and me. We are not writing the Bible anymore. That was finished when John wrote Revelation on Patmos. But when we walk God's ways, we live out His Word. As we do, we look toward that "forever time" with God in heaven.

A.D. **95 through forever**

Forever is a long, long time. Earth is a home that will not last forever. But heaven will last forever. The Lord will always be there. He invites us to come and live with Him in His wonderful home.

But we cannot go into heaven with our sins. We must come to Jesus and ask Him to take our sins away. Then we must walk with Him each day. As we do, we will get to know Him better and better. Then when we finally go home to heaven, we will go to live with a Friend.

This may be a good time for you to ask Jesus to take your sins away and be your Savior.
Would you like to do that now?